THE ACORN METHOD

The Acorn Method

How Companies Get Growing Again

Henrik Werdelin

LIONCREST
PUBLISHING

THE ACORN METHOD

How Companies Get Growing Again

ISBN   978-1-5445-0820-7 *Hardcover*

         978-1-5445-0818-4 *Paperback*

         978-1-5445-0819-1 *Ebook*

Cover Photo featuring ILEX STUDIO's Acorn Vase®

Contents

Acknowledgments

This book would not have been possible without a large group of incredible people.

First, thank you Philip Petersen, Stacey Seltzer, and Nicholas Thorne for building Prehype over the years and for being the brain trust behind our methodology. To my BARK co-founders, Carly Strife and Matt Meeker, who are the most understanding, supportive and incredible co-founders you can think of. They are building an amazing company which has not only made a lot of dogs happy, but has also created a whole new approach to business-building that we all can learn from, as you will read in the book.

I cannot thank Thomas Wedell-Wedellsborg, Mette Walter Werdelin, and Mikkel Holm Jensen enough for their ideas and advice as I wrote this book. A big thank you to Christian Budtz, Edward Roussel, Chloe Freeman, and Dan Shipper for their valuable input on the draft, and to my writing partner, Skyler White, for being the best wingwoman you could think of. Endless amounts of gratitude to the amazing people in the Prehype network who are constantly coming up with new and better ways to build new ventures, and to all our corporate partners who, over the years, have trusted us to teach them our approach to applied entrepreneurship and cocreated new ventures with us.

Last but not least, thank you to all the people who have participated in the case studies included in this book. There are too many names to mention here, but much gratitude goes out to all the amazing entrepreneurs-in-residence, partners, and corporate change agents who participated in our workshops and programs, cocreated ventures and experimented with us to help companies learn how to grow new businesses again.

Introduction

In 1964, a company in the S&P 500 stock exchange could expect to stay there for an average of thirty-three years. By 2016, the average length of tenure had fallen by almost a third. The projection for ten years on? Half that. The three most valuable companies of 2018 weren't even in 2008's top ten.

Confronted with an unprecedented amount of churn and facing shortening product life cycles and expanding fields of competition, today's CEOs and Chief Innovation Officers are under enormous pressure to find new, fast-growth revenue. Because the corporate growth toolkit hasn't changed much in the last century, they have had only two real options: improve on their company's existing capabilities or acquire another company's capabilities. Accordingly, in 2018 alone, S&P 500 companies invested a combined total of more than $1.3 trillion in Research and Development, Capital Expenditures, and Mergers and Acquisitions.

Considering this figure is thirteen times the record $100 billion the US Venture Capital industry deployed in the same period, you'd think we'd all be doing at least twice as well. In fact, each dollar invested in corporate growth today returns 15 percent less revenue than it did ten years ago. Mature companies are spending more to grow less.

I believe mature companies are like tall trees; they grow until gravity constrains them. They may shoot up rapidly, generating tiers of new branches and reaching great heights, but eventually, new growth can no longer successfully compete for resources with older branches higher up the tree.

Trees, however, don't only grow vertically. Over the last 385 million years, they have developed alternate, horizontal growth systems, enabling them to become the longest-lived multicellular organism on the planet. The famously long-lived oak, once it reaches maturity, produces acorns, a method of regeneration so successful that it has become a keystone species—one on which entire ecosystems are anchored. I believe companies, likewise, confront a natural upward growth boundary, but that they can also dramatically increase their longevity by developing lateral, offshoot companies—by creating a forest rather than a taller tree.

In this book, I argue that to survive beyond its upward growth boundary, every mature company needs to build a diversified but coherent portfolio of small, fast-growth asset companies as part of a new tree-and-forest, horizontal growth paradigm.

I call this the Acorn Method.

The Acorn Method is both a philosophical stance and a practical series of steps by which companies can propose, test, build out, and eventually integrate (or spin off) new businesses. It's the growth paradigm Amazon and Apple followed to build their retail and technology forests. It's the method I used to help build and scale companies including BARK (maker of BarkBox), Ro (maker of Roman), and the Bjarke Ingels Group. The Acorn Method gets old-growth companies back into the business of building businesses and capitalizes on the significant but often unrealized advantages they have over their younger competitors. It's something I believe mature companies must do if they're going to outlast that competition by anything like the five-to-one ratio by which forests outlive solitary trees.

I came to this realization on a flight from London to meet with three Stanford computer-science graduates who were building another photo-sharing app the world really didn't need. Seated next to me on the plane, the president of an international shipping company told me his industry sends a billion dollars' worth of empty cargo containers back to China from the US every year. In that moment, I was positioned—both geographically and philosophically—between two worlds. In one, a century-old company with billions in annual revenue and offices in more than a hundred countries had an interesting and meaningful problem. In the other, smart, ambitious, would-be entrepreneurs had a system for generating rapid growth by innovating scalable solutions for problems they didn't have. Each needed the other, and having experience with both, I founded Prehype to play matchmaker. I've spent the ten years since marrying entrepreneurial practices with corporate reach and resources, developing the structures, processes, and strategies of the Acorn Method.

As an entrepreneur-in-residence at Index Ventures, I'd worked with a wide range of startups, and was familiar enough with the tools of entrepreneurship to know they weren't a precise fit for mature companies like my new shipping friend's. Had he wanted to launch an independent startup, he would have found plenty of resources—innovation advice, business philosophies, and even step-by-step instructions—but there's little good advice available for leaders attempting to do the same within their organizations. The creation and nurturing of companies by companies is a new discipline, and there are few qualified resources. Thus, while an increasing number of organizations are realizing the importance of building a business ecosystem, they're simultaneously discovering they lack both the institutional and mental framework to found and develop one.

Most mature companies, keenly aware of the need for new growth, have sponsored accelerators, experimented with internal startups, and hired external innovation labs. These options, while better than stasis, are still problematic. Internal startups are generally expensive and slow to gain momentum. By the time the brand police sign off, HR recruits a tech team, and procurement buys in, the world has moved on, and the company is left with a large, slow, and expensive innovation nobody wants. Accelerators make for great marketing copy, but that's often all they provide. And despite their complicated coffees and so-fun foosball tables, innovation labs often launch, peak, and shut down within an eighteen-month lifecycle—hardly a compatible timeframe for large, slow-moving organizations. Despite the huge amount spent on them, most accelerators, innovation labs, and internal startups fail to produce the growth mature companies need to remain vital and relevant.

When I founded Prehype to apply entrepreneurial solutions to the problem of corporate growth and longevity, I was convinced a new paradigm was necessary—one that went beyond slapping a new digital model onto an existing analog structure. In the years since, Prehype has developed and refined a lateral growth system that builds a forest of new, offshoot businesses to revitalize towering lone-oak companies. The Acorn Method is the distillation of the system into a structure, a process, and a strategy.

- Part One: The Structure. We recommend setting up a new, quasi-independent organization or department within the existing corporate structure whose sole mandate is to build those new businesses best positioned to regenerate, support, and extend their parent company's growth.
- Part Two: The Process. We provide a well-tested, four-step process which such a structure can use to identify and validate opportunity-rich, original problems, and to create and vet multiple narrative solutions to those problems. (This process can also be used to build new businesses without the first, structural step, and we'll look at case studies of both).
- Part Three: The Strategy. Finally, our strategic component provides a roadmap for developing the most viable new business opportunities on aggressive but achievable timelines, and for managing both the immediate and long-term relationship between those new businesses and their parent company.

I've come to believe the ideal environment for a business

to build new businesses is a quasi-independent new structure purpose-built within the larger company structure. I make my case for creating such a structure in the book's first chapter (The Revenue Exploration Studio) and provide recommendations for how such a structure should be established, staffed, and financed in the second (Establishing an RES). These first two chapters are addressed to CEOs, CIOs, and board chairs who have the authority (and vision) to implement such structural changes within their organizations.

The next four chapters (Identify Interesting Problems, Articulate Possible Solutions, Create a Lean Product Plan, and Begin Signal Mining) speak more explicitly to the people charged with executing the Acorn Method's four-step business-building process which the structural component supports. This four-step process evolved first as a technique for integrating entrepreneurial practices with big company structures. It's the process and inside playbook that Prehype used to successfully grow offshoot businesses for some of the world's fastest growing start-ups and best-known Fortune 500 companies including Dow Jones, Carlsberg, Royal Bank of Scotland, LEGO, and Modelez. I've also put its practices to work at my own company, growing BARK's dog toys and treats subscription service into a forest of dog-centric enterprises.

Whether a business builds new businesses as one-off

projects or as part of an ongoing initiative to create a portfolio of new ventures, the seventh and eighth chapters provide a strategy both for managing its relationship to the larger company (Build a Runway) and for its final disposition once it reaches the end of that period (Launch Your Business). With these two chapters, I'm speaking less to the individual entrepreneur building a company within a company than to those responsible for the integration of the two.

Finally, the last chapter (Notes from the Air) is an open letter of personal advice and—I hope—inspiration. It's written to anyone using the Acorn Method to urge a mature company past its upward growth boundary by getting it back into the business of building new businesses. This approach can create limitless growth, where implemented without corporate structures to restrict it. But lateral growth systems cannot be created by or survive within rigid corporate structures any more than potted trees can grow a forest. Structure determines outcome, so that's where we begin.

Part One

The Structure

We recommend setting up a new, quasi-independent organization or department within the existing corporate structure whose sole mandate is to build those new businesses best positioned to regenerate, support, and extend their parent company's growth.

CHAPTER 1

· · ·

The Revenue Exploration Studio

The upward growth of successful organizations, like that of oak trees, slows as they mature, hence the structures that support such towering businesses are necessarily more focused on maintenance than on further (slow, expensive) vertical growth. If they are to avoid stagnation and decay, such companies must find and act upon lateral growth opportunities. To do so, they must first recognize the very structures that support their height can inhibit their expansion. While most of the CEOs and CIOs I've met with recognize that they won't get new results doing things the old way, they often still struggle to understand how very different—on a fundamental, almost existential level—today's new, post-internet companies are. To successfully compete, it's critical to distinguish among and account for the different organizing principles around which the new and old are structured.

In the same way mines are built to exploit rich seams of ore identified by prospectors, most mature, large companies today are structured not to create, but to systematically develop and capitalize on business models or opportunities initially tapped or discovered at least a generation ago. In other words, to keep doing what they've always done.

> Organizations are built to replicate, not create, results.

To return to our tree metaphor, many of today's most successful companies are currently harvesting the fruit of mature orchards planted years ago. These companies grow by expanding and consolidating—they buy neighboring orchards and transplant trees to foreign markets. I think of this as a custodial structure, and it's the way most companies were established and run until very recently.

A CUSTODIAL COMPANY

As an example, let's imagine a consumer packaged goods company we'll call Profits, Inc. Fifty years ago, Mr. Profit Senior created a popular product and built a company to manufacture and sell it. His son, Mr. Profit Junior, grew the family business, adding marketing, legal, procurement, and tech teams to support the organization, and to ensure the future would look much like the present.

To develop and manufacture a new product for Profits, Junior needed an R&D team and a factory. He needed trucks to ship it, warehouses to store it, and an ERP system to keep track of it all. Then, to sell it, he made deals with large retail companies and bought advertising on one of only a few big TV channels. Junior had to make huge up-front investments, but he didn't need to worry about competition from anyone who didn't also have an R&D department, factories, and warehouses.

Custodial companies like this, built to maintain a system and to replicate and capitalize on the results it produces, grow by making incremental improvements on their existing offerings, and by expanding the territories to which they deliver them. Such linear growth tends to produce outcomes which are consistent after a strong initial upward spike. By the time a company reaches maturity, these outcomes often include an impressive catalog of assets from resources such as patents and licensees to significant financial reserves, in addition to those mentioned in our Profits, Inc. example (factories, warehouses, established distribution and retail channels). It's a depth of resources and breadth of reach any startup would envy, but one which is nonetheless being increasingly destabilized and democratized by new technology and the internet.

SHAPE-SHIFTER COMPANIES

In contrast to the custodial organizations they disrupt, what I call shape-shifter companies grow up around rapidly changing and self-disrupting technologies and have transformation baked into their structures from the outset. Such organizations often begin as one kind of company and pivot into different fields and adopt (or create) new business models. Apple, for example, started out as a computer company. It became a music distributor when it developed the iPod; now it's a phone company. Amazon was initially an online bookseller. Today it's a movie studio and a brand that makes everything from clothes to batteries. With its purchase of Whole Foods, it entered the high-end grocery business and it's one of the biggest players in the cloud computing field. Profits, Inc., our imaginary seventy-year-old consumer packaged goods company, is still in packaged goods.

Let's say its new CEO, Ms. Penny Profits (Mr. Profit Junior's daughter), recognizes the fundamental structural differences between her custodial company and the new shape-shifter ones. Maybe in college, she had a classmate who came up with a new product idea, 3D printed a prototype, and tested it—all without an R&D

team. He then sent it to China and where it was manufactured fast, cheap, and at low volume, then shipped back as quickly and inexpensively. His artistic girlfriend designed an ad, and they bought spots on Facebook and Instagram which drove customers to Amazon Marketplace and to his website where he sold to them directly. Working with a third-party logistics company, he shipped hundreds, and then hundreds of millions of units without needing a warehouse, a support staff, or an ad agency.

From this firsthand experience, Penny knows Profits' competitors aren't just the big companies her father recognizes—they're people like her former classmate. They're also Amazon and Wal-Mart who are both now making and promoting their own products preferentially, and the tech platforms that didn't exist when she started high school. Finally, Penny knows Profits' R&D department isn't yielding the results it once did. In fact, it seems to have been hijacked by the marketing team, and is no longer experimentally developing new products at all, but simply making those tweaks to existing products that Marketing says will boost sales.

Profits, Inc. had bought several fast-growing companies in the past, but mergers and acquisitions are increasingly expensive, and it's not like Penny can internationalize again. She's stuck. The custodial structure she's inherited isn't equipped to deliver growth rapid enough to keep Profits vital, no matter how much R&D money she feeds it, but she's fairly confident shifting the company to a shape-shifter model wouldn't accelerate its growth much, and might well destroy it. Besides, going to work in flip-flops isn't something Penny aspires to. She knows better than to keep doing the same things her dad did, but she isn't going to take wild risks just to do something different, either. She wonders whether Profits, Inc. can be both stable and evolving, institutional and entrepreneurial. Are those characteristics—in organizations or in people—necessarily mutually exclusive?

Personally, I don't believe they are.

Although over half of US workers are employed by a small business, the pervasive image most people have of an entrepreneur is of the risk-seeking Silicon Valley wunderkind taking big swings for huge returns. It's a romantic idea, but an absurd one. In my eyes, an entrepreneur is anyone who solves a problem in a scalable way. It's a mindset, not a job description. No matter how large, venerable or hide-bound a company is, its founder thought this way.

Innovation is every organization's birthright.

The kind of thinking that maintains an organization is

different from the mindset that founded it. This is a good thing. I don't want banks, hospitals or airlines to think errors are interesting the way startups do. The structures which preserve institutional wisdom and which promote corporate (and often human) longevity are deliberate and elegant in their construction. They've been designed and refined over decades—even centuries—to create stability and prosperity for millions of people. We'll all be better off if these big, interesting companies—many of whom have good value systems—continue to thrive.

It's only because their survival is now under unprecedented threat that custodial structures need to be reexamined. But Penny is right; Profits, Inc. shouldn't be restructured on Apple's model. To retain and capitalize on their value, successful custodial structures must be augmented, not replaced. If they aren't—if mature companies don't find a way to enable both internal stability *and* internal disruption—they will continue to be out-run by startups and big tech companies, and I, for one, don't relish a future in which everyone gets everything they need from Facebook, Amazon, and Google.

The writer F. Scott Fitzgerald once said that the test of a first-rate intelligence was the ability to hold two opposing ideas in mind at the same time and still retain the ability to function. This is the challenge the structural component of the Acorn Method seeks to address. In much the same way that an oak tree contains a specialized acorn-generating body, the Acorn Method houses an insulated shape-shifter new-business-building structure within, but separate from the custodial structure of the mature parent company.

While the Acorn Method's four-step process of building new businesses can work in almost any corporate environment, setting up an optimized business-building ecosystem yields the best results for several reasons. Such a purpose-built structure—which we call a Revenue Exploration Studio (RES)—allows a company to build and launch new businesses in parallel rather than in sequence. It builds an internal base of experience and knowledge which benefits all subsequent ventures, and it frees the new businesses to move at startup speeds without disrupting the larger organization's longer timelines. But the most compelling argument for establishing a segregated RES inside an organization is that it helps their two different (and sometimes antagonistic) structures coexist productively.

A NEW AREA OF OPPORTUNITY

Having recognized the need for a new growth paradigm to counter the limits of mono-directional growth, a mature company might look to companies like Google, Apple, and Facebook. With their seemingly impressive ability to rapidly grow and scale new businesses, these companies are very hard to use as direct role models. Instead, from them we learn an appetite for experimentation, the ability to attract talent, and a commitment to solving their customers' problems with a range of services and products. However, they don't have a lot to teach us about moving from second-generation stability to regeneration. Additionally, their enormous financial resources make them a difficult example to follow.

Innovation at mature companies, in contrast, typically operates in one of three ways:

- Research and Development invents new technologies which the company engineers into its core products.
- Mergers and Acquisitions buys and integrates innovative new companies.
- Corporate Venture Capital, a more recent phenomenon, goes after moon shots and technology access, but mainly invests in and funds the innovations of others.

In the spaces among these three, an RES occupies an overlooked or forgotten area of opportunity where the mature company has an unfair advantage. This is where the Acorn Method works to identify what could be your next multimillion-dollar business. In the next chapter, I'll provide a very specific model for how to put these structures in place to satisfy both entrepreneurial and establishment agendas, but first, it's worth taking a quick look at two other models we've seen: the Push and the Pull models.

THE PUSH MODEL

In this model, scrappy insiders without a mandate (and sometimes against direct orders) hack their own company to do something they think it should undertake but know it won't try without prodding. These subversive entrepreneurial types often develop their shape-shifter business ideas in their free time using their own credit cards.

Authors Thomas Wedell-Wedellsborg and Paddy Miller make a compelling case for this type of entrepreneurship and feature several examples in their *Harvard Business Review* article "The Case for Stealth Innovation." In 2013, an entrepreneurially-minded member of the Wall Street Journal's "My Company Today" team had an idea he thought would be great for the company and pitched it to the only C-suite guy he knew. Unable to get much traction there, he appealed to a friend in his own department, and managed to finagle a free ad on days there weren't enough paying advertisers to fill the available space in the newspaper. After a month, he went back upstairs with some news: he had thousands of people signed up for a product WSJ didn't make. They started making it.

Such rebels are typically quite savvy and often build a plan that sketches the outlines of the product or service they'd like to see their company offer. They usually know the problem it solves, approximately how many people have that problem, the price the company could sell a solution for, and what it would cost to get it going. The most astute of these internal disruptors will have done what the guy at the Wall Street Journal did and come equipped with advanced sales, subscription sign-ups, or contracts in hand to the first conversation with their bosses.

These meetings typically begin with: "Hey, I think our business should go into the business of x. Here's what it would look like, here's how I know it will work, and here's the data to prove it, so can I please go out and do it?" They usually end with, "Yes."

Unfortunately for their organizations, such enterprising people too frequently find the corporate structure, internal politics, and resistance to change so cumbersome that they leave and start new companies of their own. In fact, in his book, *The Origin and Evolution of New Businesses*, Amar Bhide claims that 71 percent of the entrepreneurs in his study sited their previous jobs as the source of their startup opportunity.

THE PULL MODEL

In this model, a company actively seeks to draw out people

within the organization who harbor closeted entrepreneurial tendencies. In these organizations, upper management solicits ideas for new products or services the company might develop. Sometimes they offer a bounty on ideas, other times someone—usually the CIO or CEO—puts a system in place whereby people with entrepreneurial ideas can develop them themselves. Sometimes the organization will bring in a company like Prehype to run anything from a short workshop to a complete program that begins with idea development and ends by launching a new business.

At Dow Jones, for example, Chief Innovation Officer Edward Roussel established Dow Jones Springboard, a fascinating internal entrepreneur-development program which strives to surface people who have new initiatives or business ideas that Dow Jones could build within the organization.

Prehype's Philip Petersen kicking off Dow Jones Springboard

I particularly like Roussel's focus on people. Rather than looking only for ideas that senior management already recognize as good opportunities, Dow Jones Springboard runs two or three programs a year in different regions to identify and develop entrepreneurial talent throughout the company.

Brainstorming session at Dow Jones Springboard

THE REVENUE EXPLORATION STUDIO

The Acorn Method model of growing businesses within a business is a more systematized and deliberate version of the Pull Model. It establishes a separate but connected structure that gives new business offshoots enough distance from the keystone organization's long shadow to find their own light. It supports the experimental mindset necessary to identify and/or generate new opportunities, neither haphazardly like the Push Model nor occasionally like the Pull Model, but deliberately and consistently—methodologically. This structure, once in place, enables multiple paths toward the final outcome of harvesting significant financial and cultural gains from a steadily increasing portfolio of new businesses.

I first recognized the need for this structure-within-a-structure form of corporate entrepreneurship six years after founding what was then BarkBox with my two fellow dog-loving friends Carly Strife and Matt Meeker. As a pure startup happily deploying all the rapid development tools we'd acquired over a range of entrepreneurial ventures, we conceived of a fun dog toy-and-treat delivery service, tested the idea, and signed up our first subscribers before we had a product. We started packing boxes ourselves and when we looked up six years later, we had hundreds of employees, investors, substantial market share, and too many other things to do every day to kick around ideas together.

We knew we needed to create new businesses to keep growing our own, and we wanted to expand the products and services we offered our customers, but found radical new business creation difficult within our young, but by now almost corporate, organization. Internal politics and long decision cycles can leech momentum from new growth in any organization, and we found we needed different, almost mutually exclusive structures to create something truly different while also maintaining what we had.

Our customer service team (internally referred to as the Happy Team) was collecting quality insights about the problems our customers wanted us to solve for them next, but had no experience starting a new business from scratch to build those solutions. It wasn't a task for the dev team, the product design unit, or the business development group. As we spoke with other business leaders, we recognized this wasn't an unusual predicament. Few companies have internal teams to which they can turn when they want to build a new business within a mature organization.

In an early instance of what became the common Acorn Method approach, we set up an external (but connected) team charged with building a new business to address one of the biggest problems facing dog owners—dog dental hygiene. Through workshops with our science partner NovoZymes, we had identified an innovative solution and, since we felt such a venture fit neatly under BARK's "Making Dogs Happy" brand umbrella, Prehype's Amit Lubling and Steven Dean created a team to build a new business around it. We created chew toys designed to house a proprietary enzymatic tooth-cleaning gel and established a subscription service to deliver a tube of the gel and a new toy every month. Initially launched as a separate initiative called Chompers Club, it was later relaunched as BARK Bright by Mike Novotny, Mikkel Holm Jensen and their teams, and integrated into BARK's product line.

Creative, Ian, and model, Edna, from the BARK team.

CHAPTER SUMMARY

The upward growth of successful organizations slows as they mature. The structures developed to support towering businesses are necessarily more focused on maintenance than on further (slow, expensive) vertical growth. If they are to avoid stagnation and decay, such companies must find and act upon lateral growth opportunities, but the very structures that support their height can inhibit their expansion. To successfully build a portfolio of young, rapid-growth, revenue-producing new businesses, mature custodial organizations should create a Revenue Exploration Studio (RES), a quasi-independent shape-shifter structure within but insulated from the larger company.

In the same way that a keystone oak grows for decades before producing its first acorn, after years of steady—and then steadily slowing—growth, mature companies need to get back into the business of building businesses. When a keystone company wants to start growing Acorn ones, its mindset—its approach to problems, uncertainty and risk—make establishing a Revenue Exploration Studio (RES) under the aegis of, but separate from, the larger organization a structurally sound idea.

Doing so can not only produce financial gains, but also re-invigorate existing product lines and expand the company's reach into new markets. Unfortunately, most CEOs have no experience or training in establishing an RES, finding the right people to lead it, identifying areas of opportunity, or in operating and managing such an organization. Therefore, it's critical to know how to best structure the Revenue Exploration Studio to derive the greatest possible benefit to the parent while leveraging its CEO's other strengths. In the next chapter, we'll talk in detail about what we've found to be the most effective way to do all those things.

CHAPTER 2

• • •

Establishing an RES

Even for someone in senior management, getting organizational buy-in to create a Revenue Exploration Studio is hard! You're trying to do something that requires substantial resources, will certainly meet internal resistance, and is a new way of working. In the previous chapter, I made the case for setting up an RES to facilitate the financing, structure, strategy, and talent a company needs to build new revenue-generating businesses but, in my experience, some companies just aren't able to do it.

In these organizations, the senior management and boards continue using old methods expecting new results. Since you are reading this book, I'll assume that you have the ear of senior management and/or your board as well as an entrepreneurial mindset. You will need to double down on that mindset, because the first step is all about creating momentum within your organization. Many

CEOs, with an average term length of about six years, are reluctant to undertake the radical, somewhat risky, large project of creating a special purpose-built structure like an RES. The people charged with the custody of keystone companies must accept that they've hit their vertical growth limit, and that this constitutes a real and immediate danger which will require real talent, real focus, and real resources to resolve. This is often best done by creating a leadership group or committee for the RES comprised of the most senior internal stakeholders along with few external people who have startup or venture experience.

THE RES LEADERSHIP GROUP

Ideally, this five- or six-person investment and governance committee will be chaired by the keystone company's Chief Innovation Officer, Head of Innovation, or Head of Incubation. Whether this person reports to the keystone's CEO, CTO, CFO, CMO or board, or is, him- or herself, the final authority, the Revenue Exploration Studio's Leadership Group chairperson, whom we call the Studio Head, will be responsible for making high-level financial decisions, have final green light authority at pre-set milestones, and ensure the individual entrepreneur-led, new business development teams (Acorn teams) are aligned with and motivated to meet the keystone organization's goals. This studio head should have a startup and VC background. He or she should be able to offer industry and domain expertise to the Acorn teams and to connect them with relevant networks.

The RES Leadership Group should be able to direct capital to these teams and should meet regularly (monthly) to review such investments and to make decisions about portfolio balance. Additionally, the Leadership Group serves as a translation layer between keystone upper management and the entrepreneurs building new businesses within the Revenue Exploration Studio. The Leadership group performs four critical roles:

1. **Studio management:** The Leadership Group is responsible for the overall strategy, approach, and operation of the RES.

2. **Opportunity identification and testing management:** The Leadership Group provides a continuous supply of new, validated business ideas in which it wants to invest, and it hires the entrepreneurs-in-residence who develop those ideas into new businesses.

3. **Portfolio management:** The Leadership Group works with and supports all the studio's new businesses at their staggered stages of development in much the same way a venture capital associate or

partner does. Additionally, at least one member of the Leadership Group has a seat on the board of every Acorn company developed within the Revenue Exploration Studio.

(4) **Venture Operations management:** The Leadership Group further supports the RES by collecting data and best practices from all the new Acorn businesses within its portfolio and by reporting their findings both to the keystone organization and to the other new ventures within the studio.

SUPPLYING AN RES

The Acorn Method adapts venture capital practices to the ownership mindset of mature companies to encourage revenue-generating activity, to invest in the growth of that activity, and to build the systems and organizations necessary to sustain both revenue-generation and growth. With the right people in its Leadership Group, an RES executes an investment algorithm we'll discuss in the next section, and creates the ideal studio environment for the rapid creation and success of between two and four new businesses a year. To accomplish this, the RES will need its keystone organization to provide:

- An annual operating budget in addition to the funds it invests directly in the Acorn businesses.

- The active participation (not just tacit consent) of keystone senior leadership. Such engagement helps secure long-term organizational support for the innovations of the RES—support which increases the confidence of the entrepreneurs launching new ventures within it, and by extension increases their—and the RES's—odds of success.
- A clear and annually updated mandate from keystone upper management to the RES Leadership Group which explicitly delineates the territory where new opportunities should be sought and developed. This allows expertise to develop within the studio, and protects its boundaries from erosion by other stakeholders.
- The support of the keystone's legal, M&A, and finance teams.
- Investment in and the identification and recruitment of the highest caliber entrepreneurial talent.

OPERATING AN RES

PLANNING

A fully operational RES can expect to launch between five and ten new businesses in its first few years (the number of failed initiatives being much higher). Considering this, the studio head needs to plan, almost from the outset, for the variety and composition of that multi-company portfolio. A healthy ecosystem of offshoot business will be diverse in scale and mandate.

Within its bouquet of outcomes, a studio head will always look for an Acorn company to go big—even, perhaps, growing to eclipse the keystone. This, ultimately, should be the goal of your RES. The energy and entrepreneurialism of multiple young startups growing under its canopy cannot help but have a revitalizing effect on the larger organization, but iPhones outgrew Apple's keystone computer business to dramatically increase the size of its forest. A successful RES will, at worst, introduce new revenue-creating business lines for your company and, at best, do for you what the iPhone did for Apple.

Apple's Revenue

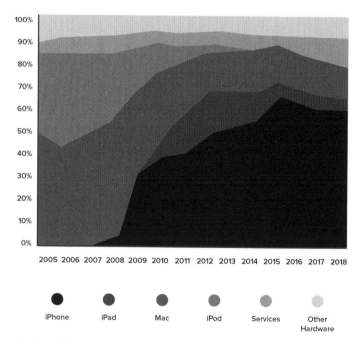

Apple products as percentage of their sales over time

A good studio head knows momentum is oxygen though and may want to start a new RES out with one or two easy ventures to demonstrate early traction, to justify the studio's creation and to secure permission from the keystone to launch more ventures.

> Find a balance between companies which are unlikely to make it at all, but could be truly transformative if they do, and those much more likely to succeed, if more modestly.

Sometimes, the studio head may need to make something that just sounds cool. The currency traded for capital and interest from the keystone is that an RES is *interesting*. It's something the CEO likes to talk about to shareholders and journalists. Alternately, if there isn't a sexy idea space within the keystone's canopy, the studio head might select an Acorn for its educational value.

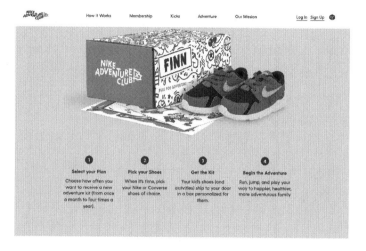

1. Select your Plan
Choose how often you want to receive a new adventure kit (from once a month to four times a year).

2. Pick your Shoes
When it's time, pick your Nike or Converse shoes of choice.

3. Get the Kit
Your kid's shoes (and activities) ship to your door in a box personalized for them.

4. Begin the Adventure
Run, jump, and play your way to happier, healthier, more adventurous family.

Nike, for example, originally launched an Acorn company called Easy Kicks (later rebranded as Nike Adventure Club). A shoe subscription service for families with children, it was created by founder Dave Cobban specifically to experiment with new ways of relating to customers that went beyond the one-off retail purchase model. Cobban and his project were so successful, in fact, that the spin-off was subsequently reintegrated.

In addition to the easy win, the big finish, the cool, and the educational, the final shade of interest the studio head can trade in is the passion project. If the keystone's CEO or some other C-suite executive is particularly fascinated by a certain topic, it's perfectly legitimate to have a related initiative in the studio's portfolio, even if it's outside the keystone's field and scope. Alternately, if there's an accomplished entrepreneur who would be an asset to the keystone's reputation or the RES's success as an entrepreneur-in-residence, the opportunity to launch a personal passion project utilizing keystone resources such as patents or specialized facilities, can be a compelling inducement.

FINANCING

Revenue Exploration Studios vary in size, but expect that, to get set up and become productive, most will require $10M–$20M annually in expenditures and investments. This is a fraction of what most keystone companies spend on R&D and other growth investments, and several million less than one quarter of one percent of the annual revenue of News Corporation—one of the smallest companies in the S&P 500. Amazon, as a point of contrast, spends 12.7 percent—$23 billion!—of its revenue on growth investments. And it shows.

INVESTING

An RES should fund Acorns on a simple model: invest growing chunks of money in those businesses which meet escalating revenue-generation targets. This may sound obvious, but a Revenue Exploration Studio's explicit commitment to exploring new revenue streams allow it to solve for revenue, and only for revenue.

Thinking and acting in this revenue-centric way concentrates investment in the highest value initiatives, primarily as a function of deselection, a technique borrowed from the VC playbook. Businesses that don't hit their revenue-generation objectives don't get additional funding. With investment, the Leadership Group makes the minimum commitment necessary, gathering enough new data at each stage to make progressively better decisions at each subsequent one.

For guidance on how much to invest at each of these stages, RES studio heads can look to the precedent offered by the venture capital industry. The VC community (for the moment at least) recognizes three stages of early investment: Pre-Seed, Seed, and Series A. While company-specific, market, and competitive dynamics can all lead to meaningful deviations from any fixed norms, according to data from Crunchbase, a Pre-Seed round of funding is typically $400,000–$750,000. Seed rounds, as of this writing in 2019, net $1M–$3M in new funds, while in the median Series A round raises $5M.

For an RES, this equates to a capital allocation "algorithm" of sorts which apportions increasing amounts of capital to those Acorn companies whose revenues hit pre-determined targets.

For example, the studio head can start by providing an

experienced entrepreneur approximately $100,000 to experiment around a specific problem thesis. If that experimentation finds adequately hospitable ground to take root—producing even just $10,000 in revenue—the RES would then automatically invest an additional $500,000 (i.e., a Pre-Seed amount of capital) to provide the entrepreneur-led Acorn additional runway for exploration and product development. If the new business continues to thrive and can convert that $500,000 into, for example, $100,000 of revenue, the RES would then automatically invest an additional amount of capital. The VC model would suggest this would be on the scale of $2,000,000. If that investment proves fruitful to the tune of, for example, $1,250,000 of revenue, the RES would invest ~$5,000,000.

This investment algorithm:

- Keeps capital efficiency and value-creation in tight focus for the entrepreneur leading an Acorn team by tying increased investments to increases in revenue.
- Facilitates rapid decision making and seamless transitions by establishing predetermined thresholds which, when tripped, trigger immediate release of the next stage of funding, increasing the successful Acorn's momentum.
- Establishes revenue as the metric against which success is measured. Because revenue is conceptually

less complicated than other measures such as user-ship or profitability, Acorn leaders can organize teams, establish performance indicators and set strategies around it.

- Creates a measurable indicator of customer satisfaction and establishes a benchmark which, if not met, will trigger the discontinuation of a project that is not working.

LEVERAGING AN RES

Investing at early stage valuations allows the keystone to own its home-grown companies for much less than it would otherwise cost to acquire a new business. This symbiotic oak-acorn relationship also advantages studio-grown startups, increasing the likelihood of their success.

Because an RES launches new offshoot business every few months, by the end of its first year, its centralized and improved decision-making will benefit every subsequent startup. Over time, the RES will also develop unique and specific unfair advantages it can deploy for each new Acorn team, and it will be increasingly well-positioned to engage superior entrepreneurial talent.

Penny Profit expected her dad, like many CEOs, to immediately recognize the need for a mature company to find new planes of growth. She understood the temptation to start small, to get one new business off the ground as a proof of concept which would then secure the permission to build more, but Mr. Profit immediately understood the reasons for establishing the first entrepreneurial team within a Revenue Exploration Studio. He wanted enough at-bats to have good odds at one of those multimillion-dollar startup homeruns, and he knew the difference between one trip to the gym and an exercise regimen. He was on board. With the important first step of establishing an RES behind it, Profits, Inc. committed to exploring the areas of opportunity where it had an unfair advantage, and hired Penny's former classmate-turned-entrepreneur to head up their new Revenue Exploration Studio.

CHAPTER SUMMARY

Establishing a Revenue Exploration Studio sponsored by, but separate from, a mature organization begins with upper management buy-in, the identification of areas of unfair advantage, and the recruitment of a stellar leadership team. It is then supplied with both an investment fund and an annual operating budget, as well as with institutional support and other resources.

Once set up, an RES draws down capital and invests in new business ventures according to an algorithm that ties an Acorn's ongoing funding to its revenue. Using a process we'll detail in the next four chapters, the RES develops, tests, and refines new business ideas approximately every three months to create a portfolio of new businesses that leverage the sponsor organization's strengths and return significant financial and cultural gains.

With her former classmate at the head of Profits' newly established and funded Revenue Exploration Studio, Penny and her company were ready to get into the business of building businesses. What they needed next was a problem.

Part Two

The Process

We provide a well-tested, four-step process which a structure can use to identify and validate opportunity-rich, original problems, and to create and vet multiple narrative solutions to those problems. (This process can also be used to build new businesses without the first, structural step, and we'll look at case studies of both).

CHAPTER 3

• • •

Identify Interesting Problems

With a Revenue Exploration Studio (RES) established, the Acorn Method moves from structural concerns to questions of process. With the one-time work of creating a business-building structure within Profits, Inc., Penny—or the studio head she's put in place—now needs a reliable, efficient, repeatable process tailored to the identification, articulation, presentation, and evaluation of new business ideas. The Acorn Method's four-step growth process is optimized for business-building inside an RES, but I've used it successfully on projects as diverse as creating a new kind of retail store for Chanel to developing a new business line for my own company. Over the next four chapters, I'll take you step-by-step through the process and give you all the templates and examples you need to build a business from scratch.

PROBLEM FINDING

Most people think of problems less as things to go in search of, and more of those things which find you despite your best efforts, but try a thought experiment with me: Imagine asking the next two people who walk into your office for five innovative business ideas. They'll most likely answer with questions if they respond at all. Now, imagine asking them for five business problems. They'll talk until you run out of coffee. Some innovation agencies fetishize it, but ideation is the male oak flower of the Acorn Method, and problem-finding, while less showy, is the true site of Acorn formation.

Not only does problem finding yield more immediately productive and fertile territory than attempts at idea creation, it's also where most startups had their origin. Many entrepreneurial ventures are grounded in problems their founders faced, solved, and sold to others. The founders of Airbnb ended up revolutionizing the travel industry after renting out air-mattresses in their own apartment. Sara Blakely solved her underwear problem and made $11 billion on Spanx. The Acorn Method borrows this entrepreneurial angle of approach, and adapts it to existing organizations which are, in fact, often better situated than they know to address the problems they face once they stop seeing them as things to eradicate, and start looking at them as the potential springboards they are.

> A well-defined, interesting, and meaningful problem is at the root of the best new businesses.

As an established company, you have an advantage over the rogue proto-entrepreneurial problem-hunter. Your territory is discreet and defined, and you're already deeply knowledgeable about it and its inhabitants. Leveraging this institutional wisdom positions you to move quickly from your business problems to your customer's problems. Surface and resolve new problems for the people you already serve, and your relationship with them will expand and deepen. And it'll be more profitable, too.

This problem-before-solution approach is exactly the reverse of the way most mature companies undertake expansion. Most invest in the research and development of new technologies, innovating first and then searching for applications. Alternately, they identify exciting new technological advances that other companies have made, and search for applications in their own field. The Acorn Method, meanwhile, challenges companies to put people first. Identify a human problem, and then develop technologies, products, or services to solve it. Too often, technology is a solution in search of a problem. Finding the problem first greatly reduces the costs in time and money of matching customers with your solutions.

It also demystifies innovation. There's a great deal written about ideation and creativity, and plenty of innovation labs are happy to take on this work for a fee. Because, unlike most innovation labs, Prehype is run by experienced entrepreneurs who expect to build what we come up with, the Acorn Method takes a more practical approach. Because it's easier for people to think about problems than it is to come up with new ideas, we don't try to come up with ten ideas for each of six problems. It's much more productive to look for just three ideas for twenty problems. Accordingly, the first in the four steps in the Acorn Method's business-growing process is problem finding, and our first exercise is to finish the following phrase: "It sucks that..."

Designed for problem-finding, our "It Sucks" notepads have a range of applications.

> Force yourself to come up with hundreds of different problems.

COLLECTING COMPLAINTS

When Prehype works with a company to start growing offshoot companies, we've typically been invited in by the CEO, company owner, or innovation lead who's responding to at least some of the pressures we explored in chapter 1. At Prehype, we usually start with a workshop for a group of ten to twenty. Identifying the right people to involve in this process is part of my personal area of expertise so for me, it's mostly intuitive. If you're starting this process within your own company however, ask yourself: "A year from now, who are the people most likely to have left to start their own companies?" Enlist them. They have the entrepreneurial traits that will make them successful at this work, and involving them with it is a great employee retention plan.

Once you have your group assembled, ask them to finish the sentence, "It sucks that..." Usually, this will first yield a list of things that are problems for the individual person or for the company. That's fine. Let workshop participants get that out of their systems, then remind them of two critical constraints: the goal is to find interesting problems *that you can solve*—no flying cars or time machines, please—whose solutions might be something *that people would pay for.*

FINDING PERMISSION

In the same way that an acorn will only flourish within the same general environment of its parent tree, companies have the most success growing new companies in adjacent market spaces. These areas are those where, even if you don't already have one, your presence will still make sense to consumers. If you're a video rental company, starting a streaming service is an obvious—but adequately distant—area of expansion. If you're a toy manufacturer, making computer games is still a connected space, even if it's culturally a little further afield. That said, I love the thought experiment of asking: "If Nike made a hotel, what would it look like?" and "If Hilton made a shoe, what would it be?" Some brands have permission to play across a wider territory, and others do not. If you don't have a clear sense of the size of your sandbox, don't worry. Disney probably shouldn't open a string of surgical centers, but your company's playing (and Acorn-growing) field is probably broader than you think it is.

When consumers have a specific problem they're trying to fix, they don't care what kind of capability is needed to solve it. If, for example, you're a plumbing company, and a guy calls wanting you to fix his clothes washer, he doesn't care that the issue is electrical, not plumbing. He wants to do his laundry, and he wants you to be a problem-solver who is very good at fixing anything in his house that uses water.

> Where do you have permission to play?

In determining those areas where your company has permission to play, you're specifically looking for those places where you have an unfair advantage. These are those areas where you have better brand recognition and more ready access to consumers than other newcomers, and where you'll be able to leverage your company's experience and institutional wisdom. You likely have permission to play anywhere you have patents, licenses, sales reps, or other resources already in place that would allow you to move more quickly or with less friction than your competitors.

Having delineated the boundaries of the lateral growth web where you have permission to play, you can now start tapping it for interesting problems. I like to conceptualize this as drilling down through any of five borehole questions:

- What business are you actually in?

- What are your customers telling you?
- How might you preemptively disrupt yourself in places where you're vulnerable to external disruption?
- What's changing in the wider world that might create opportunities in your space?
- What issues would the different stakeholders in your area pay you to take care of for them?

THE REDEFINITION BOREHOLE

Broadly speaking, there are two ways a company can think about what it does. First, it can define itself by the utility it provides—it's a financial services company, or a retailer, or a logistics company. This is certainly the most traditional, and by far the most prevalent view, but I think it's shortsighted. Remember, all companies originate to solve a problem. The utility a company now provides is the solution it once developed—helping people manage their money, or connecting consumers with manufacturers, or getting products where they need to go. This is second way of defining the business you're in—shifting your focus from the utility you provide to the problem you solve—can reveal a long, lateral vein of places where you have an unfair advantage and permission to play.

Redefine your business by the problem it solves.

When you define a company by the problem it solves agnostic of utility, Disney is in the business of creating magical entertainment for kids and their parents. Google's remit is organizing the world's information. Had we defined BarkBox by its utility, we'd be in the dog treat and toy delivery service. Seen through the longer, problem-solution lens, we're in the business of making dogs happy. Not only is this redefinition a lot more fun, it immediately suggests possible offshoot businesses. All we need to do is look for other ways to please a pup.

When Dow Jones, the parent company of the Wall Street Journal, redefined the business WSJ was in from its utility—producing newspapers—to its purpose—disseminating business-critical information—it experienced a similar expansion of possibility. As a business information company, it was providing a distillation of business world news and presenting it as actionable data that business people needed to do their jobs.

This broader company definition encompasses many terrifically interesting problems, some of which led to the development of exciting offshoot businesses which ranged from developing risk and compliance services (under the stellar guidance of Chris Lloyd) to building mobile and web apps like Newsmart.

Newsmart, a 2015 WSJ collaboration with Harper Collins, bundled their online "newspaper" with a tool for teaching business English to non-native speakers. The image here is from the fourth of Acorn Method's four-step process, Signal Mining, which chapter 6 discusses in detail.

THE LISTENING TO CUSTOMERS BOREHOLE

The internet revolution changed the business landscape in thousands of ways, but to my mind, one of the most profound was the radical shift in the expectations customers have about how a business interacts with them. Once, for the communication between a company and its end users to be anything but one-way, customers needed to call a one-eight-hundred number or write actual letters on paper. Today, they can leave online, public reviews of a business, post to its Facebook page, tweet about, text to, and email with it. And when they do, they expect to be heard.

While there are downsides to this new higher-touch way of interacting with customers, it's great for problem-finding. BARK built a very successful product line called Super Chewer as a direct response to hearing our customers' frustration with how quickly their dogs destroyed toys. It was an easy-to-identify problem that BARK solved by designing fun toys constructed of non-plush materials for very active dogs. Our Listening to Customers borehole yielded a great business idea, free market research, and goodwill from a customer base who felt heard.

THE SELF-DISRUPTION BOREHOLE

Often, during the "It sucks that..." exercise, a specific set of anxieties shows up around external threats. These are often places where people inside a company sense that competitors are poised to move into adjacent spaces in ways that will disrupt it. The people may not initially be clear on what form that disruption will take, but probing more deeply into this subset of found problems can yield interesting opportunities. As an example related to the previous borehole, the disruption I see posing the greatest threat to most companies today is the risk that one of your competitors will capitalize on the internet's power to build a more direct relationship with your customers than you have. I think if you don't currently have strong, one-on-one, web-mediated interactions with your customers, you are in real danger of facing the same fate that befell Blockbuster when Netflix created its more direct relationship with Blockbuster's customers.

THE ANTICIPATION BOREHOLE

If the previous exploration springs from anxiety about future disruptions and the desire to take defensive action, anticipating opportunity-creating changes in the world motivates a more exploratory list of problems. Sometimes, companies find there's a new technology emerging with possible applications for their existing business. Other times, there are early signs that society is changing in a way that opens up new territory or new demands their products or services could satisfy. Offshoot businesses that grow up along this lateral have the potential to expand the company's range, and to increase the places where it has permission to play.

You don't have to search to find companies impacted by changing technology. The iPhone gave rise to a wide range of entirely new companies from TaskRabbit to Uber, but it also opened up spaces for existing companies savvy enough to recognize an opportunity when it appeared on the horizon. Unity, for example, began life as a 3D modeling software. Almost coincidently, it was also a great engine for building iPhone games, and when a demand for that repurposing of their technology became apparent, Unity was smart enough to advertise it. In the

B2B space, Zendesk anticipated the need businesses would have to manage inbound emails sent to their support departments, and had a product ready.

THE INVESTIGATION BOREHOLE

The final lateral to explore for interesting problems within the areas where you have permission to play grows from an exploration of the stakeholders with whom you're already involved. Here, you deliberately go looking for big, meaningful problems that such people would happily pay you to solve. If you can identify an urgent problem shared by many such people, solving it makes a terrific basis for a new business.

The Royal Bank of Scotland, for example, had a problem. They were collecting fines and bad PR because their customers were signing documents they didn't understand and sometimes hadn't even read. This was a problem for the bank, not their customers, so it didn't immediately qualify as a lateral opportunity. Working with Prehype's Meeta Gournay, the bank reached out to other organizations in their industry, and quickly learned everyone was dealing with the same point of pain.

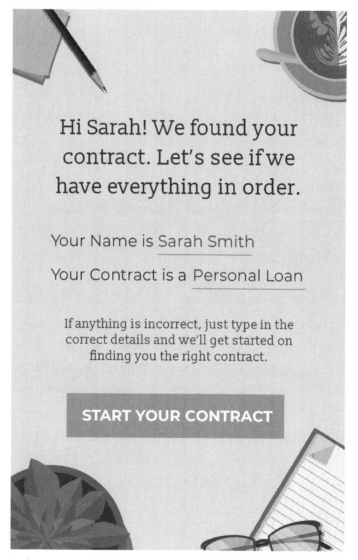

SAFE TO SIGN

Hi Sarah! We found your contract. Let's see if we have everything in order.

Your Name is Sarah Smith

Your Contract is a Personal Loan

If anything is incorrect, just type in the correct details and we'll get started on finding you the right contract.

START YOUR CONTRACT

Early prototypes of Nift's UI

⊘● ⚐● ✐● **SAFE TO SIGN** ☰

1 Personal Loan   2   3   4

Sarah Smith's Personal Loan

This document contains all the personalised information for your particular agreement, for example how much you're borrowing and when you need to pay it back.

1 The Loan 〉

1.1 The Bank will provide the Customer with a Loan for the Customer's general business purposes and pay the Arrangement Fee.

1.2 The Bank's Base Rate Loan Terms form part of this Agreement and are available to be read and printed online. Alternatively, a copy can be obtained from the Customer's Relationship Manager.

See Overview Text ▶

✓   ▤

Working with a team of experts in artificial intelligence, the Royal Bank of Scotland developed software that walks bank customers, point by point, through the terms of their loans. Customers got a detailed explanation of what the contract they were signing involved, and banks got proof of their informed consent. The Royal Bank of

Scotland not only solved a problem for themselves and their customers, they created a new software service, Safe to Sign, which it eventually spun off as Nift to provide related solutions to many other companies in the banking services space.

Sometimes, a company already has expertise in a function which it can leverage into a wider, saleable service for its entire industry. In the 1950s, American Airways discovered (with the help of IBM) that their ticketing system was not only unique but superior to what other airlines were using. They built a new company, Sabre, around that system which still exists today as Expedia. Amazon, for a more recent example, famously used its sophisticated data warehousing to create Amazon Web Services.

CREATE PROBLEM STATEMENTS

Having identified areas where you have permission to play using the five boreholes above, you next need to open up the laterals they reveal. Use the prompt, "It sucks that..." and have workshop participants write their answers on sticky notes. This approach helps keep people focused on problems rather than on ideas. Problems let you target solutions, ideas drift toward daydream. People typically enjoy responding to the prompt, and a group of ten to twenty can easily generate hundreds of sticky notes.

In a room of domain experts, there will be a certain amount of overlap in topic or theme, so in the next step of Identifying Interesting Problems, we put all the sticky notes up on the wall and get a sense of the range of issues they cover. Often, between five and ten main topics emerge which we gather into topic clusters. From this group of related complaints, we compound a problem statement, typically cutting hundreds of sticky notes down to just a few meaty problem statements.

As an example, when BARK in collaboration with its biotechnology partner Novozymes went problem-finding along the Redefinition lateral, we shifted our focus from the utility we provided—dog toys and treats delivered monthly—to the problem we solved: We help dog lovers make dogs happy. Then we started filling in the blank.

For people who want to make dogs happy, it sucks that

_____.

At the end of that session, among the notes on the wall were: "dogs have bad breath," "80 percent of dog gets oral disease," and "it's expensive (and no fun) to clean a dog's teeth." We clustered these mouth-themed problems and came up with a compelling problem statement: "Dogs aren't getting the preventive dental care they need which negatively impacts their health and happiness." If you love your dog, that'll get your attention. There are an estimated 525 million pet dogs in the world, so we had an important problem inside our area of expertise that many people would probably pay someone to solve. We thought that someone should be us.

PROBLEM REFRAMES

Having found an interesting problem and articulated it as a problem statement, it's tempting to jump straight into looking for answers. I'm sympathetic with the impulse, but there's an intermediary step I'd strongly encourage you to take. Pioneered by Thomas Wedell-Wedellsborg, an advisor to Prehype, Problem Reframing opens possibilities that were initially invisible. You might reframe the problem that dogs aren't getting adequate preventative dental care to focus on the lack of a fun or even simply a hassle-free way of caring for a dog's teeth. Preventative dental care for dogs is tedious. Then ask: What can we do about that?

Reframing shifts perspective.

Perhaps my favorite example of a problem reframe leading to a less expensive and more elegant solution is one from Thomas Wedells-Wedellsborg's wonderful book *What's Your Problem?* A building management compiled a list of related "it sucks that" responses which included:

"The elevators in our building run too slowly," "People get impatient waiting for the elevator," "Our tenants are complaining," and "Elevator retrofits cost millions of dollars."

This cluster of complaints led to a juicy problem statement. Importantly, this wasn't: "We need an inexpensive way to make our elevators faster." That was the building management company's problem. A well-phrased problem statement focuses on the end user, so here, it was: "Our tenants need a faster way of moving between floors." This led to several good reframes, one of which surfaced the underlying problem: People are bored waiting for the elevator. Having stated and then reframed the problem, the final question: "What can we do about that?" led to an elegant, effective, inexpensive answer—mirrors in the elevator lobbies. Without changing the speed of the elevators, they satisfied their tenants whose waits felt shorter with something interesting to watch.

Problem + Solution = Idea

Identifying and reframing a host of interesting problems yields, almost by default, a generous number of actionable ideas. On the curve from nothing to something, you now have the first half of several possible good ideas for new businesses.

The next step is to go from an idea to a narrative solution you can vet.

CHAPTER SUMMARY

The Acorn Method's four-step growth process begins by identifying interesting problems using the "It Sucks That" exercise along laterals opened up through four area-of-permission boreholes: redefinition, listening, self-disruption, and anticipation. The output is then rendered as problem statements which are reframed to create actionable new business ideas.

Penny, a group of internal domain experts at Profits, the newly hired Revenue Exploration Studio team, and a few of Penny's entrepreneurial friends spent several hours exploring what sucks for their end users. They discovered it sucked that:

- Their packaged goods required expensive and eco-logically unfriendly packaging
- The logo and brand colors which made them recognizable also looked dated
- Most of their products were associated with unpleasant household chores

Focusing even more tightly on the various stakeholders who interact with Profit's products, the team imagined how their customers and distributors might say "It sucks that:

- The product doesn't fit in my pocket when I need to use it on the go."
- I feel guilty about adding plastic waste to the world."
- My kid can open the product without asking me."

The list went on and on, but the idea emerged that Profits, Inc. might leverage their existing infrastructure to develop an organic line of artisanal household cleaning products in biodegradable packaging that included aromatherapy oils and which would match a new line of luxury hand lotions. The team went out for dinner that night and came back the next day ready for the second step in the Acorn Method's process stage, articulating possible solutions.

CHAPTER 4

. . .

Articulate Possible Solutions

Congratulations, you have problems! Because you've reframed them, you also have ideas. At this point, you may find it very tempting to start writing business plans or building prototypes, but those are time-consuming undertakings which can eat the momentum you generated by moving quickly through problem-finding and reframing. It's critical to move equally quickly through first developing and then eliminating possible solutions.

This development and subsequent elimination are the second and third steps of the Acorn Method's quick-growth process, and in this chapter and the next, I'll be diving deeply into them. This material, while not overly technical, will be of more interest to individual entrepreneurs, their teams, and members of the Revenue

Exploration Studio Leadership Group than to senior leaders inside the keystone. Readers in positions like Penny's might skip ahead two chapters to Signal Mining—the fourth process step—as it's a valuable way for both them and the teams they lead to validate new business ideas.

To quickly expand and evaluate the problem statements developed in the first step, identifying interesting problems, entrepreneurs next need neither a business plan nor a prototype, but stories—narratives of possible solutions. You will eventually pick the highest quality one or two with the best odds of success, but to get to quality, you must have quantity. We see this same lesson reflected in the wisdom of oak trees. A single keystone oak can produce up to 10,000 acorns with the expectation that most will be eaten by everything from chipmunks to turkeys to bears, fall victim to rot, or fail to reach hospitable soil.

> Momentum is oxygen.

The Acorn Method has a useful template to help people move quickly through creating not solutions, but stories about possible solutions. Solution narratives built on this template have four other significant advantages in addition to being faster and less expensive than other testing grounds.

- They put the focus on the story-telling component from the outset since there's compelling evidence that entrepreneurs who start with the story of their idea raise money whereas those who start with detailed explanations and business models don't.
- The narrative process helps refine and clarify the core idea. It's easy for the "why" of a new business to get lost in the process of working out the "how," and by keeping the problem clearly in focus, you avoid the drift that can cause a new company to end up with a solution nobody needs.
- By insisting on a restricted number of slides, the template forces clarity of thought and expression.
- Building thirty or forty solution narratives makes it more obvious which ideas aren't worth pursuing further.

As odd as it sounds, your goal during the entire four-step process phase of the Acorn Method is to kill the ideas you're trying to build. This stance, which we call "default dead" means that, up to the point of launch, you're not trying to prove you have a good idea; you're trying to falsify your thesis. Creating a short solution narrative provides a great first stress-test that can surface what would become fatal flaws before you have much time or any money invested.

A solution narrative is simply the story of a problem and

its solution. It's a neat and concise expression of your thesis statement designed to test the power of your idea in much the same way Hollywood vets a movie concept before they commission a screenplay. Called an "elevator pitch" because it needs to be short enough to deliver in the time it takes to ride an elevator, it also needs to be compelling enough that, by the time the doors open, the studio exec wants to hear more.

Pitches are a before-and-after Cinderella story of the problem your product or service will solve. If the problem is that dogs need to have their teeth cleaned but everyone involved hates tooth brushing, the solution would be a fun way of preventing dental disease by cleaning a dog's teeth. At this point, you don't need to know how you'll take customers from cinders and soot to glass slippers and ball gowns, you just need to capture the emotional power of the transformation—of their problem meeting your solution and living happily ever after. The "why" power needs to be present at this point and to stay in focus throughout.

Elevator pitches are short, in part because movie executives have short attention spans, but more significantly because future ticket buyers do, too. Likewise, you'll have about the length of a movie trailer to interest potential customers in your product, and you won't get much longer to pitch the business behind it to a decision-making executive.

Because the goal is to eliminate all but the best ideas, it's important to move rapidly through building your pitch. In our workshops, participants go from a qualified but intangible idea to a complete, share-able, concrete pitch in a single day. They're able to do this because we've developed a template to capture and articulate the most relevant components of a great pitch. The Quick Pitch is six slides of mandated large type (72-point in PowerPoint, 37 in Google Slides) to keep you focused and encourage brevity. People often have trouble being concise when they pitch, but ideas are clearest when stated simply. Or, in the folksy words of Woody Guthrie, "Any fool can make something complicated. It takes a genius to make it simple."

THE QUICK PITCH

The Quick Pitch template is a set of fill-in-the-blank sentences which you use to make a genius-simple, six-slide pitch deck for each of your twenty or so best ideas. This template concisely distills the story of your problem and solution and neatly articulates the core of your business idea. In addition to serving as a quick litmus test of idea quality, it's also the first step in building your case for why your keystone company and/or its RES should invest in this particular idea. It should generate enthusiasm and get management eager for you to move forward. Let's break it down:

THE PROBLEM IS...

The first sentence states the problem you've identified. Whether its impetus came from responding to your customers, redefining the business you're actually in, or any of the other boreholes we've discussed, this is where you compellingly and succinctly spotlight your interesting problem.

> The problem is dogs need better oral hygiene, but they and the people who love them hate brushing their teeth.

> The problem is your options, when trying to get a car to drive you to a destination in your city, are to stand on street and play a game of luck or to call your local car service and hope they can help you right away.

INTRODUCING...

The second slide is two words: "Introducing" and the proposed name of your company. This is the hero moment and creates drama. You've stated a problem and said you are the answer.

> Introducing BARK Bright

> Introducing Uber

_____ IS A (WEBSITE/APP/SERVICE/COMPANY/ PRODUCT) THAT...

After you hooked your audience with your great problem and interesting product name, now you can explain what your solution is. Here, you provide only the information they most need as simply and in as few words as possible.

> BARK Bright's Canine Club is a subscription service that makes it easy and fun to build a life-long habit of caring for your dog's teeth.

> Uber is a car service which allows you to book a car from wherever you are, track its progress to your location, verify its driver's identity, monitor the route to your destination and pay for your trip all from within an easy-to-use app.

IT WORKS LIKE THIS...

The fourth slide satisfies the curiosity your audience will be feeling now that they know what you're promising. In fewer than three lines, you explain how your solution solves their problem.

Canine Club works like this:

- You go to our website and tell us what kind of dog you have.

- We send you a kit with a toy, a gel, and a tooth-cleaning enzyme.
- You put the gel in the toy. Your dog has fun with the toy, and you've taken care of his oral health.

Uber works like this:

- You open the app on your phone, enter your pickup location, select among available cars and book one.
- You track the driver's progress to your location, verify the car and driver against the app's photo and description and, if you choose, monitor the route driven against the app-recommended one.
- Once you reach your destination, you simply exit the car. Payment, service fee, and tip are dealt with in the app after the driver has left.

WE MAKE MONEY BY...

If you were simply trying to pitch a great solution to an interesting problem, you'd be done at this point. Because the Quick Pitch is designed to also pitch a solution to the problem of business regeneration, the rest of the deck is focused not on your future customers, but on the people to whom you need to sell the idea of the company you're proposing to provide that solution. The first of these pitch-the-business slides tells decision-makers what they most want to know.

We make money by charging a monthly subscription fee.

We make money by charging drivers a fee to use our system and receiving a percentage of the payment for each trip.

WE WILL GET OUR FIRST CUSTOMERS BY...

This slide further builds the business case for starting a company around your solution narrative.

We will get our first customers by marketing to existing BarkBox subscribers.

We will get our first customers by using our network of friends who travel a lot.

OUR VISION IS...

Now that you've made the pragmatic argument for building this new company, your pitch needs to reground itself in emotion. The second-to-last slide, a statement of vision, should recall the interesting problem you set out to solve and provide an inspiring picture of life with your solution in place.

Our vision is to protect the oral health of the dogs you love with fun toys to chew on every month.

Our vision is to be the premier car service in all the major cities of the world.

THANK YOU

The final slide leaves your audience with a powerful, succinct restatement of the entire pitch. It provides your proposed company's name, its tagline or verb-noun slug*, the idea kernel and a thank you.

BARK Bright
Toys that treat dog teeth
Thank you.

Uber
Everyone's private driver
Thank you.

*The verb-noun slug is a technique Prehype teaches in workshops as a valuable tool for making certain, early on, that there's a clear value proposition behind any idea you're going to invest time developing. This imperative sentence has "you" as the unspoken subject, addresses the customer, and captures the action you want the customer to take. As an example, the verb-noun slug for YouTube would be "upload videos."

THE QUICK PITCH REVIEW

The Quick Pitch is easy to assemble, but it accomplishes a great deal. It focuses thinking, clarifies the proposed new venture's purpose, and creates a tidy package of what was previously a diffuse collection of thoughts. It also allows for a true one-to-one comparison of ideas. Having tapped into interesting problems, reframed them, and created Quick Pitches for approximately twenty of your best ideas, you're in a great position now to step back and evaluate what you have.

Often, it's immediately apparent that there's a good deal of overlap among several of the pitches. Rather than twenty or thirty completely unique narratives, there are two or three variations around ten or fifteen significantly different themes. Clustering and consolidating these performs the first round of eliminations.

Until this point, your focus has been on creativity and generation, but here you switch into a more critical mindset. It's important to qualify the ideas that will go on to the next stage, creation of a Lean Product Plan, because it requires a more significant investment of time and the first financial resources you'll be expending on building a new business. With the goal of winnowing your ten to thirty Quick Pitches down to between three and five, evaluate them all on three criteria.

IS IT POSSIBLE?

We eliminated the flying car ideas at the outset, but often there are compelling solution narratives to interesting problems that are still unrealistic in scope or technology. If Tesla didn't have a radically improved battery, or if Canine Club didn't know there were enzymes that cleaned dogs' teeth without brushing, those pitches would be eliminated here.

IS IT FOR US?

Although you always start looking for ideas by defining the places where you have permission to play, you need more than a territorial claim to justify further investment in an idea. You want to pursue only those ideas where you have a unique and significant advantage. Unlike a startup, your company already has resources and leverage on which your new venture can and should capitalize. Eliminate any ideas that don't make good use of your unfair advantages.

IS IT JUICY?

This final metric is the most subjective, but often the most telling. To move on to the next stage, an idea needs to make people hungry. If nobody in your organization is excited enough by an idea to want to start working on it, if it fails the gut check, if no one is sufficiently driven by the need to have this product or service available to advocate for it, cut it now. Moving from idea to action requires dedication and commitment, and an idea that meets all the pragmatic criteria but fails the passion test, fails.

CHAPTER SUMMARY

In the second step of the Acorn Method's process phase, multiple ideas uncovered through problem-finding and reframing are rapidly developed and articulated as narratives of possible solutions by using an eight-prompt template. The resulting Quick Pitch is then reviewed and the best two or three selected to move on to the next step.

After all the Quick Pitches have been made, only a few should be selected to move forward, after further development, to the next round of pitching. In my experience, if you pitch five ideas, you end up with two, and if you pitch two ideas, you still end up with two. People seem to have cognitive difficulty thinking of more than two or three big ideas, but are reluctant to drop down to just one. Often, there will be a clear choice—a sensible, moderately safe idea—and, almost in contrast, a more extreme, risky idea that may be less likely to succeed but has the potential to be disruptive and exciting. Senior management, in these cases, usually sign off on both. That willingness is helped, in part, by the limited scope of what signing off on a Quick Pitch means. It still doesn't mean expensive prototypes and time-consuming business plans. Rather, the Acorn Method's next process step involves another template and another incremental but powerful extension of possibility and validation.

...

CHAPTER 5

Create a Lean Product Plan

On the journey from nothing to something, creating a shareable account of how your concept will help solve a meaningful problem in a scalable way is, in my view, one of the most impactful but undervalued exercises you can undertake. While building such a presentation isn't complex, when you get this step right, you have an easier time securing support for your project and moving it past the "I have a good idea" stage. The specific format we developed—the Lean Product Plan (LPP)—is relatively quick to make, consistently delivers powerful results, and forms the third step in the Acorn Method's process. An LPP is approximately thirty slides long, consists of five sections, and will serve as the foundation for the next stages of development.

Much in the way Hollywood couches an elevator pitch in language like "Imagine a world where..." the Quick Pitches you develop should tempt the imagination. An LPP builds on that initial spark of interest. Like an entrepreneur's version of a screenplay and storyboard, it provides a visual, detailed, and even more compelling picture of what your proposed new venture promises customers, investors, and staff and helps you clarify for yourself what you're trying to create.

Here again, our method borrows from its namesake nut. Because they are too heavy to be carried an adequate distance from their parent trees by the wind, acorns have evolved to be very attractive to scatter-hoarding animals like squirrels and jays. Likewise, LPPs are designed to entice and to function as a kind of "Social Object" to which people will be attracted themselves and motivated to share with others.

THE LPP IS NOT A BUSINESS PLAN

Business plans are plans, not realities, and the numbers they contain are often based on assumptions not facts. Nevertheless, when tasked with writing a business plan, most people suffer an almost irresistible urge to turn to Excel. The hero of any story told in Excel is inevitably the finance person. The finance person then turns to the idea person and questions him or her about numbers which are, by necessity, inventions. These conversations quickly bog down in the relative legitimacy of alternate (but equally made-up) numbers, and the entire process can become mired in what is essentially an absurd conflict.

An LPP addresses the business case for your innovation-based business while avoiding the unnecessary detours than can arise when you're talking about how a product that doesn't yet exist will perform with customers you don't yet have. In my experience, your audience needs to believe that your solution will solve a problem common to a large group of people, and that it's built on business fundamentals that makes it scalable. Making a convincing case on both fronts requires a mixture of storytelling, data, and consumer insight.

At this point, it's often most efficient to move the project along dual tracks, simultaneously developing the visual and the business components. This can, of course, happen sequentially, but the LPP isn't complete until you have both. Your LPP is the only selling tool you have at this stage of the process, and the better it looks, the more likely it is to persuade. I firmly believe it's well worth investing in quality design at this juncture. You don't have to spend a lot, but you'd be well served to earmark a budget for professional design to help bring your vision to life. More than any other part of your pitch, design makes your proposed venture feel real. If you don't have a design team on whom you can draw, an online freelance site like Upwork can be an excellent and cost-effective resource.

HOW TO BUILD AN LPP

Like the template for the Quick Pitch, the Acorn Method's LPP template is a series of prompts and fill-in-the-blanks that guides you through the creation of a slide deck. The template is designed to sequence and present necessary information in a way that captures and holds the imagination and that creates a sense of a *fait accompli*. Throughout, you'll talk about your new company as though it already exists because you want the audience, at the end of your presentation, to be left wondering why it doesn't. Your promise, at that point, is that it can—quickly and inexpensively.

SECTION ONE: INTRODUCTION, INSIGHTS, AND PROBLEM

The first part of an LPP provides the context and insights your audience needs, and sets the stage for the problem statement. The information included here often recalls the initial borehole you went through in problem-finding to communicate the pain points you'll address.

Examples:

- Language-learning textbooks are incredibly boring for adult learners, especially business people.
- People don't understand the agreements they sign with banks, leading to mistrust and lawsuits.
- Many dogs develop oral disease before their third birthday because they and their owners hate tooth brushing.

An LPP should include several such insights which should be tweet-length and relevant. It can be helpful to preface them with an indication of how many people have the problem you're addressing, and you can include the "It sucks that" where appropriate.

Examples:

- Business English is the fastest growing professional language-learning area in the world, with about 60 million people taking such classes at present, and growth projected to reach 100 million by 2030.
- On average, a person will agree to between twenty-five to seventy-five legally binding agreements, from mobile phone contracts to iTunes user agreements to loan paperwork.
- More than 90 percent of dogs will develop severe oral disease in their lifetimes.

Next, in two more tweet-length statements, clearly and crisply state the specific problem your concept solves.

Examples:

- With English as the lingua franca of an increasingly global marketplace, non-native English-speaking businesspeople need an engaging, modern way to learn business English.
- Dogs need the same kind of preventative dental care we give our human children, but there are currently no trusted, quality products available to make it easy for their owners to do so.
- Bank customers, intimidated by the complexity and legalese, frequently sign agreements without reading them, creating a liability problem for banks.

SECTION TWO: SOLUTION

The first slide in the Solution section recalls the Quick Pitch. It begins with "Introducing _____" after which you fill in your proposed venture's name followed by a pithy description fewer than six words long.

- Introducing BARK Bright—Bad breath is a big deal
- Introducing Safe to Sign—Helping consumers understand their legal documents

Having said who you are and what you do, the next slide explains how. Here, a return to storytelling works well. Briefly walk through the customer's journey beginning with a description of your prototypical customers, how they first encounter your product or service, and their sequential interactions with it. You're connecting the problem you've articulated with the function the company services.

- Lucy loves how cuddly her toy spaniel is, but Speck's breath has gotten so bad she's stopped wanting him to sit in her lap. Luckily, one of her friends tells her about Canine Club. Lucy goes to our website, tells us a little bit about Speck, and picks the plan she wants. When Lucy gets the box, Speck thinks he's won the Best Dog prize. He loves the tooth toy and wears himself out playing with it. Now, he's ready for snuggles and, with his clean mouth and reek-less breath, Lucy's happy to scoop him up and enjoy the real win of good dog health.

- Ethan is excited to be taking out his first business loan, but, even though he knows his way around a profits and loss sheet, he can't make sense of the contract he's been asked to sign. Impatient to get back to building his business, he signs without reading and is stunned when his first payment comes due a month later. Ethan vows never to borrow money again, but then he hears about Safe to Sign (Nift). Knowing he'll be guided through the process, he's ready to expand his business again.

Finally, you conclude the Solution section with a recap of the top three benefits your product or service provides for your example customer.

- To recap, Lucy and Speck get a great toy every month, better oral health, and more cuddles.
- To recap, Ethan feels he had the time he needed to understand the elements of the agreement, that he better understands his risks when taking the loan and that his bank helped make sure Ethan got the answers he was looking for.

SECTION THREE: BUSINESS

If the first two sections of your LPP pitched your new business's new product or service to potential customers, the last three pitch the venture to the executives able to greenlight and fund it. Here, you need to give your audience a sense that is a viable business at scale by providing the very basic unit economics of your suggested business.

First, you'll provide the business case, ballparking an alphabet soup of metrics: the CAC, LTV, PPU, TAM, and COGS.

- CAC: What do you estimate it will cost to acquire a customer?
- LTV: What is the lifetime value of that customer?
- PPU: How much do you expect customers to pay for the product or service?
- TAM: How many people do you believe have the problem you're going to solve?
- COGS: How much will it cost you to produce that solution?

Customer Acquisition Cost (CAC)

CAC means the average cost of acquiring one customer, and it's primarily used in the context of marketing (or acquisition) where you can calculate your ad spend against the number of customers it brought in. Your company probably already has some benchmark numbers, but you can also find the CAC ranges for different product categories online or run some simple experiments online to find a realistic range. CAC is expressed as a dollar amount per customer ratio: $\$x$/User. In the next chapter, I'll give you a quick way of getting real data to estimate your projected CAC.

Lifetime Value (LTV)

The LTV answers the question: how much will a customer spend over the duration of their relationship with your product or service? Commonly given as a key performance indicator for subscription-based services, it can be used more broadly. At this early stage, it can be hard to determine an exact figure here, but an estimated range based on comparable LTVs you find online or within your current business can be helpful. LTV is expressed as a simple dollar amount although it's helpful to indicate the expected time frame as well: LTV = x (y years)

Price Per Unit (PPU)

Here, you want to account for: how much customers will pay for the product or service, whether there are tiers of pricing or levels of service, and whether customers make a one-time purchase, pay a monthly subscription fee, and/or replace consumables. In short, the PPU number tells your audience how the money comes in and from where.

Total Addressable Market (TAM)

Your TAM number is an estimate of how many potential customers you expect for your new product or service with particular attention paid to how that number might grow over time. Note that there can be several types of customers over time. Initially, you might have customers of only one type or industry. Later, a broader range of people might benefit from the solutions as well, allowing your product or service to expand to serve those customers as well.

Example: In the LPP for BARK Bright, we included the following figures about our Total Addressable Market:

- There are 525 million pet dogs in the world.
- This number has been rising steadily across the globe.
- In the US alone, 42 million households have an average of 1.4 dogs.
- And increasingly large percentage of dog owners think of their pets as family members and feel strongly motivated to care for them as such.
- We believe that we can reach approximately 10 percent of US dog parents in our first two years.

Cost of Goods Sold (COGS)

To determine your COGS number, you're looking at the actual cost of traditional production and operations, without regard to the development costs. This number helps determine the potential profit margin of the product once the business is established. Your company probably already has models for solving for this number, so be prepared to explain how your business might differ (or not) from those models.

Later in the process, we'll add another abbreviation: NPS (Net Promoter Score) which will track potential customers' responses to the question of how likely they are to recommend your product, but the goal here is to come up with approximate figures. Your goal in providing these numbers is to give your audience enough data that they can begin to engage with the business idea on a nontheoretical level. Data provide an effective stepping-off point for conversations about the business, as the audience now has pragmatic questions it can pose to itself such as: Is that the right price per unit? Could it be higher? What if we're only able to reach half the suggested addressable market? What if I think we can get to more?

Four Additional Questions

The Two-Year Projection

Based on these assumptions about the number of customers, product mix, and pricing, what is your revenue likely to look like two years from now?

The Go-To-Market Plan

How will you acquire your first customers? Do you have a master plan for repeatable access to customers and distribution?

The Competition

What other options are available to your customers to solve this problem? How are you different?

The Advantage

What are the advantages the parent company has that will benefit this new business idea? Are there resources such as infrastructure, customer access, knowledge, and datasets that the existing business has which could help accelerate the new business?

SECTION FOUR: VALIDATION

At this point in your LPP, you're no longer pitching your idea, new product, or service. Instead, you're trying to sell your audience on providing the resources you'll need to move forward into the Acorn Method's fourth process step—Signal Mining (which we'll cover in the next chapter).

The purpose of Signal Mining is to test the assumptions and validate your concepts, so here you pitch the need for that kind of validation by spelling out two things. First, what assumptions you plan to test, how you plan to test them, and what results would prove your assumptions valid. And second, the timeline and cost of that testing.

Assumption Tests

Assumption tests are designed to surface the bets you're making and the main hypotheses on which your proposed new venture relies. These are the assumptions you'll need to prioritize proving or disproving.

For each of up to three of your foundational assumptions, complete the following:

> We are betting that our (customer or product or service) has this (hypothesis of problem).
>
> Action plan to test that hypothesis:
>
> - []
> - []
>
> Results that would validate that hypothesis:
>
> - []
> - []

Example:

> We are betting that **dog owners are concerned about their dogs' oral health**.
>
> Action plan to test that hypothesis:
>
> - We'll conduct fifty interviews with individual dog owners across the US to gauge how concerned they are about their dogs' oral health.
> - We'll run several online advertising tests to see how

many dog owners interact with messages focused on dog oral health.

Results that would validate that hypothesis:

- Of the fifty interviews, at least 50 percent of respondents rate their level of concern at a four or higher on a one-to-five scale where five is the highest level of concern.
- Our online ad tests achieve a 5–7 percent click through rate.

Runway and Resources

Finally, detail how much time and money you'll need to validate these high-priority assumptions, establish who will execute on the LPP and validate the hypotheses, and explain why your team is the right team to build your proposed new business.

SECTION FIVE: CONCLUSION

The concluding section quickly summarizes your pitch and reconnects your audience with the initial excitement they felt. Sometimes the big idea energy gets lost in the process of building a solid business case for its realization. Now, with their doubts allayed and questions answered, you remind your audience of the inspiring "why" behind your well-reasoned "how."

Where Might It Go from Here?

Provide a picture of the future and of how early success would open up new possibilities for the new business and for the keystone organization. Think of the LPP as proposing the first of what could become many new ways you can help the specific customers your new venture is being established to help. As an example, the LPP for BARK Bright might suggest that if we're successful with our dogs' oral care product, we would be well-positioned to help out with dog owners' other health-related concerns. We could develop a natural tick repellent or anti-gas chews, painting a picture of the different ways we could grow to become a dog health company.

Why Us?

Summarize the unfair advantage the parent company has as the founder of the new venture by demonstrating how there's a strong fit between it and the problem you're solving, the product you're proposing, or the market you intend to serve.

Pitching a dog's oral health product to BarkBox, I'd point to our large customer base as an enormous unfair advantage. Additionally, there's a great deal of institutional knowledge about how to communicate with dog parents, which we could both capitalize on and add to.

What's the Vision?

In a final, tweet-length statement, summarize the big idea behind the new venture.

PRESENTING YOUR LPP

If you've taken the dual track approach, by the time you've assembled information to complete the above template, you're probably starting to get the design components in place. Now it's time to put it all together and prepare your pitch. It's a vulnerable position for any new venture to seek buy-in when there's nothing tangible to buy, and anyone you're likely to pitch to at this point is more inclined to say no than yes. Therefore, it's critical that your presentation be flawless and your audience carefully chosen.

Never end a presentation with a yes-or-no ultimatum. Instead, take a "What will it take to get to a yes" approach. Because your goal in delivering your LPP is to understand what it will take to get buy-in, solicit feedback and tough questions. Getting buy-in usually involves presenting not just to key stakeholders, but their teams and other people with whom they want to consult about your idea. In these conversations, you'll learn when it is appropriate to build on the organization's strengths and when to point out what in your new venture is different or new and needs to be dealt with differently.

A good presentation is as much theater as it is information session, and poor delivery of excellent material is equally (if not more) likely to fail as a powerful presentation of weak material. Over the years, Prehype has developed a set of best practices that I recommend you follow—or, more accurately, worst practices I recommend you avoid.

PRESENTATION PROHIBITIONS

Don't wing it! You are giving a performance. Rehearse for it. Practice your presentation until you feel completely comfortable, and then audition it for others. When I'm preparing a pitch, I'll test it out on anyone who doesn't walk away—my friends, the guy in line at Starbucks with me, my dog, etc. Knowing you're well-rehearsed will improve your odds of success and help quiet your nerves.

Don't ad lib. If you're not a stand-up comedian, stick to the script. You've put a great deal of time and deliberation into making sure it's as strong as possible. You've reviewed the numbers and the language, and designed each piece for maximum impact. Nothing you come up with on the fly is going to be as powerful.

Don't think you know everything. Listen to the feedback and questions. Sometimes it's better to listen and work to uncover the underlying concerns, than to jump to the defense of your idea. Try to understand the goals of the people to whom you're presenting. Is your project aligned with or diverting them from their goals? If the latter, how will you address that?

Following these recommendations will help you give a great presentation. That won't matter if it's not delivered to the right people.

PRESENTATION ATTENDEES

Ideally, you've been engaged in an ongoing conversation with the person or people who have the authority to greenlight every stage of growing an offshoot business, but if not, you've now gone as far as you probably can without buy-in from upper management.

Your position at this point is subtly different from that of an entrepreneur looking for outside investors. First, potential stakeholders within your organization are more inclined to be supportive. In some instances, they may even have a mandate to create new businesses like the one you're proposing. Even so, they likely also have constraints, and strategic and budgetary concerns an outside investor wouldn't. Depending on the scope and purpose of your proposed venture, your presentation will likely be targeting one of three levels of buy-in: local management, business, and executive.

When you're pitching a specific sponsor within your organization, your presentation needs to be less complex, less formal, and will likely be delivered one-on-one. Business level buy-in becomes necessary when you're pursuing technical, communications, or HR support—or when the idea you're pitching isn't an exact fit for any one person or internal team. Ideas that are large or outside of the company's core strategy require executive level buy-in. Here, you'll be presenting to more people and will need to provide more complex and detailed information. Regardless of which audiences you're pitching, make sure you understand and address the concerns and limitations specific to them.

SELECTED SLIDES FROM THE LEAN PRODUCT PLAN FOR BARK BRIGHT

The Problem:

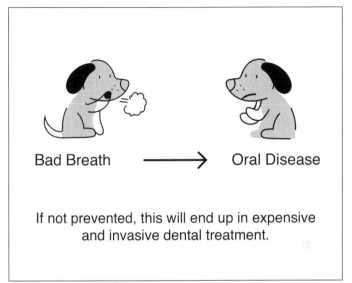

Bad Breath $\longrightarrow$ Oral Disease

If not prevented, this will end up in expensive and invasive dental treatment.

The Solution:

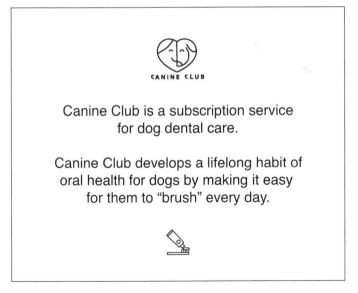

CANINE CLUB

Canine Club is a subscription service for dog dental care.

Canine Club develops a lifelong habit of oral health for dogs by making it easy for them to "brush" every day.

The Business Case:

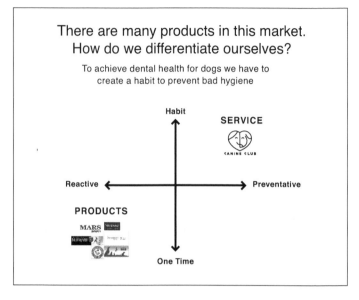

Validation:

Conclusion:

Thank You!

CHAPTER SUMMARY

Moving from ideation to creation in the third step of the Acorn Method's process phase represents the largest investment yet of time (and the first of cash) to create a Lean Product Plan. This professionally designed and well researched deck of approximately thirty slides compellingly presents the problem, solution, and business case of your new venture. It then spells out what resources are needed to validate the ideas and test the assumptions on which it is based, and leaves its audience feeling excited about the new venture's possibilities.

Lean Product Plans are visual, detailed, well-researched, informative, persuasive, and much less likely to send people down Excel rabbit holes than the typical business plan. Building an LPP and using it as the backbone of a presentation to internal stakeholders is the best way to get buy-in from the people who will fund the next phase of your new venture's development. It's also the primary tool for that next phase, the fourth and final piece of the process phase—Validation.

The gist of your LPP presentation is: "We've discovered an interesting problem, articulated a possible solution, and presented how we believe that solution might be useful to customers and profitable to us as a company. We'd like to build an offshoot business around this potentially rewarding solution and, to reduce the cost of trying, we're asking for time and money to test the assumptions we've been making."

The Acorn Method tests assumptions and validates market demand with a process called Signal Mining. It's an elegant, efficient way to determine the viability of your proposed business, estimate the cost of growing your customer base, and establish organizational priorities. It also saves you from working for years on a product that your customers don't really care about and offers, perhaps, the Acorn Method's greatest return on investment.

CHAPTER 6

. . .

Begin Signal Mining

The odds that any given acorn will become a tree are a disheartening one in ten thousand. While a new business built with our process has much better odds than most others, innovation *is* still risky, and leaders are rightly cautious. If companies are going to grow a forest of off-shoot businesses, they can't gamble on acorn odds, or even startup ones. New business ideas need to be tested to validate their viability.

> To lower the risk of innovation, reduce the cost of trying.

In big companies, it can take tremendous effort just to get a manager into a meeting room, much less excited about something. So if you've managed to generate enthusiasm with your LPP, it can be tempting to just grab as much money as you can and run with the idea. Additionally, inspired by the more software-focused lean startup movement, people often think starting out by building an MVP (minimum viable product) is the right choice. The MVP is a cornerstone of the lean startup movement and, for most people, means pursuing the most stripped-down, quick-and-dirty version of your product you can get out to customers. But what's the MVP for a new type of satellite truck? MVPs are great for some new ventures, but for most of the projects I've been involved with, you can get key user insights without actually building anything first.

It's an understandable impulse to want to dive in but, like an oak tree, you need to play a long game. The Acorn Method's victory condition isn't launching a solitary offshoot business; it's lowering the institutional resistance to innovation. To do that, you need to put some resources into making sure you've identified the right problem, developed the right solution, and that the right number of the right people will be willing to pay you the right amount to solve it. There are a lot of variables you need to validate.

SIGNAL MINING

Signal Mining is the Acorn Method's process for refining a new business concept and validating market demand for a product or service before substantial resources are committed. Not a whiteboard or academic market-sizing exercise, Signal Mining is a "boots on the ground" field study that yields actionable data. It's the final step of turning interesting problems into a qualified business opportunities and, depending on the strength of the signal you find, it will become part of the first step in the strategy phase of building your new business.

To avoid letting momentum drop during the final step of the process phase, plan for one or two people to take about a month to complete a round of Signal Mining. Costs will vary, but even if you hire an outside company to conduct the process for you, it shouldn't be such a significant investment that you'll be constrained to a single round. Speed and efficiency are the primary considerations, but as an estimate, budget at least a thousand dollars but not more than fifty in printing costs, time, and ads to drive traffic. Likewise, there isn't a standard sample size for Signal Mining. We'll talk more about levels of engagement in a second, but because the strongest signal is a sale or a purchase agreement, if you're testing a new jet, a sample size of one pre-order would be enough to justify moving on.

Signal Mining reduces the cost of trying.

To get the full value out of this process, it's important to undertake Signal Mining as an iterative loop rather than a one-off activity. Setting up an experiment once, and then evaluating and learning from the information you collect might render a simple yes-or-no verdict on the feasibility and potential profitability of your idea, but because Signal Mining is faster and cheaper than building an MVP, you can get better than binary results. You can retest much faster, improving both your offering and its odds of success. Even with only a few customers providing feedback, you'll be able to iterate your way to a product or service capable of making a significant impact on a real problem your customers are motivated to address. You can think about this loop as an E^3 triangle.

- **Expectation.** Design your experiments to accomplish two goals: to test the assumptions on which your plan's business projections are based, and to increase your odds (or at least your confidence in the odds) of its success.
- **Execution.** Conduct your experiment in the real world on real potential customers or clients. In an endeavor as speculative as dreaming up new business ventures, signals are practical, concrete, actionable measures of facts, not theory.
- **Evaluation.** Measure your experiment by two criteria: Effectiveness (did it return useful information?) and output (what data did you collect about your

ability to reach potential customers, about the degree to which you've identified an acute problem felt by a core group of them, and about their level of interest in your proposed solution?)

When we were developing BarkBox, we had assumptions about how many subscribers we could expect to sign up. To mine for a signal on this, we put together a picture of a BarkBox webpage, which I then took to a dog park. I showed people the screenshot of what the website would look like and asked them, if I built this box for their dogs, would they buy it?

The first questions they asked were consistently: "How much would it cost?" and "What would be in it?" Our first experiment had taught us that cost was an important factor and that the webpage needed to show a sample box. Since we had established that there was enough interest to warrant another round of experimentation, we went around the E^3 triangle again. This time, we created a box mock-up, added pictures of it to the website, set the price at thirty dollars, and off I went to the dog park again.

This time, people reacted positively to the offering and the price, and when I asked my, "If I built this" question, they said, "Sure. I'd sign up for that once it's ready." Stopping there would have been a good signal, but the best indication of whether people will pay in the future for your product or service is that they'll pay for it in the present, before it's available. When people signaled they'd be interested, I tested further for that ultimate signal. My co-founder Matt Meeker had Square on this phone, and we could offer to swipe credit cards and take preorders in the moment. People who show polite interest become very honest about how good they think your idea actually is when it's time to turn over their cash.

> Spending sends the strongest signal.

With sixty-eight dogs signed up, we had a signal strong enough to justify building an actual website.

HOW TO MINE FOR SIGNALS

Having gotten buy-in on your LPP, you asked for modest resources to test the assumptions on which that plan was based, and to further refine your new business idea and validate market demand. Now, you're going to develop the experiments you think most likely to deliver the information you need to feel confident going forward. This information will vary depending on whether your proposed business follows a business-to-consumer (B2C) or a business-to-business (B2B) model.

In the first round of Signal Mining, you should go pretty

low tech. Take a screenshot of the best slide from your product plan and, using a service like Instapage, create a landing page that announces you'll be launching soon. The page also serves as a way to get emails from those interested in being notified when it goes live. Experiment with different channels—Facebook or Instagram ads, targeted emails to existing customers—to drive traffic and evaluate interest.

Signal Mining on Facebook for a data about the cover and title of the book you're reading. We wanted to test which headline and front cover people would prefer. Instead of just guessing, we designed five different covers and added four different headlines and then ran ads on Facebook to see what people clicked on the most. This allowed us to move away quickly from guesswork and, with data in hand, feel more comfortable about which cover and book title to use.

The number of visitors to the landing page from different sources will tell you about the efficacy of your advertising and about the level of interest in your identified problem space, while the number of email addresses you collect measures interest in your proposed solution. A service like Google Analytics can also give you more detailed information about the behavior and demographics of the people who signed up and those who visited.

Signal Mine Questions to Answer:

- Have you identified a problem that generates consistent consumer need?
- How much will it cost to find such consumers and acquire them as customers?
- Are there enough such customers and are those customers willing to pay enough to support viable per-unit economics?
- What features or benefits matter most to these customers?
- Can you get your product or service to market quickly enough to reasonably expect those numbers to still be relevant?
- What data would significantly increase the confidence and excitement of your stakeholders?

DESIGNING SIGNAL TESTS

To return actionable data, a signal test needs to be carefully designed to answer an empirical question. A good question asks quantifiable things like: how much, how many, by when, and at what cost?

Once you've established the signal for which you're mining, but before you begin, you need to determine:

- **Who to ask.** Your target audience might include current customers, consumers in adjacent markets, suppliers, manufacturers, present business partners, current clients, or secondary stakeholders. In creating your LPP, you identified potential customers and clients. This is where you go to Signal Mine. You're testing the premise that enough of this population will be willing to pay you enough to make the venture financially viable.
- **Where to find them.** You might reach the audience you've identified through your own network, through colleagues, social media, or advertising. For B2C projects, you can simply go where your audience is likely to be in the same way I took my website mock-up to the dog park. For B2B projects, a phone call is usually the easiest path to a signal. When we needed to measure the signal from business units outside the Royal Bank of Scotland, we called their general managers, explained the service, and asked if they anticipated wanting to use it.

- **What to show them.** We'll discuss signal distortion later, but for now it's enough to recognize that Signal Mining isn't a survey. Asking an audience directly for the signal you're seeking fails to return actionable data because self-reporting is famously inaccurate. The number of people who resolve to lose weight at the start of each new year, and the number of people who weigh less by the year's end aren't even close to the same number. Because present behavior is the best indication of future behavior, we're looking for signals that closely replicate or anticipate what people will do, not what they say they will do. Create an opportunity for your target audience to take action—direct them to a landing page, event, pilot, presentation or video.

- **What to capture.** Measure verbs—purchase, sign up, subscribe, click, or interact. You may also be able to capture qualified metadata which is more accurate than self-reporting. Finally, you can and should capture any written or verbal inputs, less for the input itself than because the act of writing or speaking indicates at least a nominal level of engagement. It's very possible to get reliable responses to questions of opinion or preference. More respondents might report a desire to purchase than will actually buy, but the percentage of people who say they'd buy red over blue, and the percentage red and blue sold won't differ as dramatically.

- **How to output your findings.** It's important to format the data in a way that highlights the answer to the empirical question you've been Signal Mining to answer. Depending on the data you've collected and the stakeholders to whom you need to communicate it, your output might be a spreadsheet, a presentation, a graph, a statement document, or a detailed report.
- **What other utility might you derive?** Beyond signaling interest in it, watching potential customers or clients interact with your proposed product or service can help you better target your offerings, prioritize features, and avoid mistakes. It can also reveal what other data might increase the confidence and excitement of your stakeholders thus helping shape your next round of Signal Mining. It can also indicate where a new direction might produce a stronger signal, and we'll talk more about that next.

HOW TO MEASURE SIGNAL STRENGTH

The strength of a signal is measured by the number of interested people and amount of permission they're willing to give you. We recommend starting small. Early signal strength tests can include an exploratory conversation in person, over the phone, or by email. They can also include Google and Facebook ads, mockups, and landing pages. If a reasonable percentage of people are willing to give you a verbal or written "I'm interested," or better yet, indicate that interest by giving you their email address, you can escalate to asking for a stronger signal—an indication of intent. For a B2B venture, this might involve discussion of terms or a letter of intent to become a client. For A B2C venture, you want to see that the price you're proposing doesn't cause a precipitous drop in interest, but that interest persists beyond the introduction of price.

Having established interest and intent, you have permission to ask either for payment (in B2C operations) or a signed contract for payment (in B2B ventures). The strongest signal is a large number of people who have already entered into a customer or client relationship with your business before it's been built.

You're likely to see some decrease in the number of people as the level of engagement increases, but regardless of where the line starts on the left, a line that ends high on the right—having either risen steadily or started high and fallen only slightly—will give the strongest signal.

SIGNAL DISTORTION

Beyond the unreliability of self-assessment and prediction, two other factors can skew a signal: politeness and alienation. Pitching friends and strangers your new business idea is great practice and may help you refine the way you talk about the product and the problem it solves, but the level of their enthusiasm should not be mistaken for a strong signal of future sales. I call this the "cocktail curse" because I've never had a negative response to a new business idea from a friend over drinks.

The phenomenon extends beyond bars. People, in general, like to encourage new ideas and tend to respond with enthusiasm to your excitement. Here's how the curse plays out: Tell a friend you're thinking about starting a service that will deliver her morning coffee so she doesn't have to stop at the coffee shop on her way into work. You can even qualify your audience by making sure she likes a coffee in the morning and stops for one on more days than not. Odds are, your friend will be supportive. She'll love the idea and encourage you to make a go of it. What she says will almost certainly be polite. Then ask for her coffee order and credit card. What she does next is a signal.

On the opposite end of the friendliness spectrum, focus groups may allow you to observe unsubtle behavior from behind a painfully obvious one-way mirror, but they do so in an environment so artificial it distorts results to the point of unuseability. In my (perhaps cynical) mind, it's not only the artificiality but the economics of focus groups that make them suspect. I think most focus groups return the results that the company paying for the focus group wants to see. Signal Mining is less biased and more realistic—future customers who will buy your product online are online looking at your product. It's also more efficient, more accurate, and more affordable.

To avoid distortion and to get an accurate measure of signal strength, your tests should be more of a sales pitch than a research request. People are much freer with their opinions than with their cash, and your company's future health depends on a diet of the latter. There's an enormous difference between: "I'd like your advice on my startup idea," and "Hey, I have this product, do you want to buy it?" The conversation changes when you ask for money, but since that's what you're eventually going to have to do if your business is going to survive, that's the question most likely to deliver a distortion-free, actionable signal.

FOLLOWING A SIGNAL

Sometimes, in the process of Signal Mining for a proposed product or service, you discover a much stronger signal for a different application of your core idea. At Prehype, for example, I once worked with two very talented entrepreneurs who had identified an interesting problem that housing co-ops had trying to coordinate the people who lived in their building. The team had worked up a wireframe iPad app and were taking it around to co-ops mining for a signal that would indicate enough interest to warrant building out the idea, but they'd been getting a fairly lukewarm response. People could see the utility of the software, but they weren't on fire to buy it and put it to use solving their problem. The problem the entrepreneurial duo was solving wasn't causing potential customers enough distress to generate interaction-level interest. Building managers were telling the guys: "I don't really need this in my co-op, but I'd love to have it in my office. Can I have it for that?" They were smart enough to say: "Absolutely!"

They went back to work and made what was wanted.

The team was smart enough, yes, but because they were recruiting customers for a product they hadn't already sunk months and money into building, they were also able to be flexible. They retooled the app to track office rather than housing concerns and got a much stronger signal. Managed by Q became an operating system for offices instead of co-ops, and sold in the spring of 2019. The original co-op app would probably have done okay had it not refocused, but Signal Mining the concept before planting and developing it allowed the seedling company to reach much greater heights.

While Managed by Q shifted its customer base to follow a stronger signal to a more profitable "who," Signal Mining can also help refine your "what." We had this experience field testing an idea developed in collaboration with a company in the entertainment space. Prehype's Oliver Rechnitzer and his team were getting a weak signal for our solution but consistently hearing the magic words, "if only" from potential customers. If only our product could solve a similar problem—one we hadn't identified, but which our potential customers were feeling very strongly about—they'd sign a twelve-month contract that day. We hadn't designed or built that feature, but because we also hadn't built any of the ones we had designed, it was a few days' work to sketch it in, mine for what was now a very strong signal, and launch a product for which we already had purchase commitments. Skill Up went on to fulfill its strong initial promise as a startup called Reppio.

Introducing Reppio

A mobile app and platform managing your event staff

A strong signal is about as close as you can get to a guarantee of success. If you find many people ready to interact with your idea, build it. If there's a strong signal from a different audience or for a different function, follow it. But what if there isn't a strong signal at all?

OUTCOMES

At Prehype, we make ideas to Signal Mine test all the time. Here are a few that never became big ventures, but from which we learned a lot about a certain set of problems and, with the first, learned how to make lollipops too!

Stephanie Roland and Casper Willer, two Prehype entrepreneurs-in-residence, tried to set up an online business selling organic lollipops. They were great lollipops—they used only whole foods, contained no refined sugar, and people loved them.

They sold well at farmer's markets and festivals, but when we ran a simple Signal Mining test against taking them online, we discovered the model broke down at the cost of customer acquisition. This early feedback allowed the founders to move on to new projects, instead of putting more time and money into something that wasn't viable.

Another time, in the wake of one of the big storms that hit New York, I thought people might want to buy disaster preparation kits, so I built a simple landing page to test the idea. The low cost of driving a great deal of traffic to the site was promising, but of the twenty-thousand people who visited, only a hundred signed up. Clearly, a need was there, but my proposed solution wasn't meeting it.

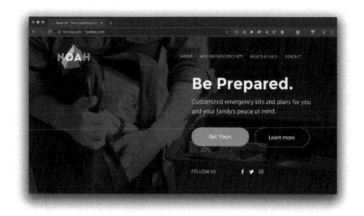

Finally, sometimes you'll take a project out looking for a signal and in the first week know it's never going to work. People hate it. The silence is deafening. This is still a success story. Discovering the lack of signal at this stage saves a team of people from investing tens of thousands of dollars and years of their lives trying to tango with a corpse. Don't keep investing and iterating trying to grow an acorn on stone. It's demoralizing and keeps you from tending more promising plots.

Both a strong positive signal and the total absence of one make the next step obvious: you go operational in the first instance and in the second, you shut it down. Much of the time, however, the signal is present but weak, rendering a verdict that's much less clear. There's no direct translation from results to next steps in such a scenario, and entrepreneurs and their sponsor organizations tend to address it from subtly but significantly different agendas.

In old oak companies, inertia can slow forward movement—sometimes just short of the point where an idea would start to flourish, whereas the unrooted entrepreneur's momentum may carry an idea forward past the point of diminishing returns. My advice in both instances is the same: bias your decision *against* your natural inclination. I coach early stage startup companies and corporate ventures alike to quit and start again absent a strong signal. That said, if you're cultivating a forest, and your enthusiasm is much stronger than the signal you're getting back, keep going. Your job as an internal innovator is to move the organization forward, and here, I believe, it's better to nurture less robust growth than to let it die too easily. Crispin Porter's former Chief Creative Jeff Benjamin often says: "Making is thinking," and I think that is a good mental model for new initiatives. Certainly, don't start a new company without a solid signal, but if your keystone-sponsored business has survived to this point, it's worth running more rounds of the iterate-and-test loop before giving up on it.

Perhaps the best metric for an Acorn team at this juncture is this: after Signal Mining, do you have more or less confidence in the viability of your project? It's a subjective measure, but if you're honest with yourself, I suspect you'll know if your project fails the gut check. If it does, confess your disappointment, shut it down, and go back to problem-finding. If, however, you're still convinced that you have at least the kernel of something promising, it's your job to pitch it, even without the numbers you were hoping to have. Go back and update your LPP. Find a new spin on it and go mining for a fresh signal.

Follow your confidence, but not too far. It's possible to stay in the iterate-and-test loop long enough to lose your bearings. If, after a few go-rounds, you're still not seeing much of a signal, don't fall prey to the sunk cost fallacy. It's still better to quit on a dead seed than paint it green and sew leaves on it. There's no shame in stopping. You haven't failed, and the extra investment hasn't been wasted. You've undoubtedly learned things and acquired skills that will increase the odds of your next venture's success.

> The only resource you can't recover is time.

You have a limited amount of time in your career to invest in building businesses, and there are opportunity costs to every attempt. However, actually making each attempt is an education equivalent (or superior to) an advanced degree. Beyond that, it's about as much fun as you can get paid to have. The process of innovation is exciting and intrinsically valuable. When you remind yourself of this and affirm it to others in those instances where it's not also extrinsically rewarding, you prove yourself an innovator—one who innovates. That's the victory condition—for you and for your organization.

> **CHAPTER SUMMARY**
>
> Signal Mining is as close as you can get to guaranteeing success. It identifies potential revenue streams, and establishes who your new business's customers will be and that they actually want what you're proposing to offer them.

The Acorn Method's four-step business-creation process concludes with Signal Mining and, with strong indication of good market fit, and with your LPP's assumptions validated, you're ready to transition from idea to action and go operational. Whether your new venture required several iterations or got a strong signal of viability from its first test, once you have one, you've successfully made the almost alchemical shift from nothing to something, from tree (big company) to acorn (new business idea). The second shift is the one after creation, growth—going from acorn (idea) to plant (a new company)—requires germination.

Real-world acorns need the right conditions—loose, moist soil at least twenty meters from the parent tree—and time to establish their single taproot which can grow to depths of six feet before a single shoot breaks through the ground. During a new venture's equivalent period of extraordinary and rapid change, the new business venture is equally reliant on the right strategic environment—a secure runway at a carefully chosen proximity to its sponsor company. In the next two chapters, the Acorn Method leaves the business-creation process and moves on to growth strategies. Chapter 7 is mostly concerned with strategies for creating that runway while chapter 8 covers what happens as an Acorn starts down it.

Part Three

The Strategy

Finally, the Acorn Method's strategic component provides a roadmap for developing the most viable new business opportunities on aggressive but achievable timelines, and for managing both the immediate and long-term relationship between those new businesses and their parent company.

CHAPTER 7

· · ·

Build a Runway

Moving out of the Acorn Method's four-step business-building process and into operational strategy always feels like crossing a threshold to me. No matter how many times I've taken a business from idea to launch, I always have a moment where I ask: "Am I really going to do this? Am I ready to take this solution out into the world and start trying to solve that problem for an increasing number of these paying customers?" It's one thing for a tree to grow an acorn, it's another thing altogether to find out if the acorn can grow on its own.

Whether developed inside a Revenue Exploration Studio or as a one-off special project of a larger organization, a company-grown new venture often finds this inflection point marks the boundary of their sponsor's comfort zone. The Process steps can feel more like intellectual play than real work. They cost very little and are more abstract than concrete. Because taking the business live changes all that, it's critical to have a strategy both for the transitional period and for the different possible final outcomes.

The Acorn Method's unusual process, with its focus on problem-finding, pitching, planning and verifying, differs from most business-development ones because it's been aiming at this moment since it began. The RES structure is different and the growth process is different because you're not stopping at the usual endpoint, you're going operational.

The shift from conceptual to operational is, for me, where things get most interesting, and where real value is created. During the Acorn Method's third phase, the focus on experimentation, on testing and iterating remains, but there must be a strategic shift in commitment, in timeline, and in the interaction of the new business venture and RES, to create the best conditions for success.

DESTINATIONS

With a strong signal of customer interest, and having validated your assumptions about what your product or service will cost to create, and what the market is willing to pay, you know a great deal more than you did at the outset, and much more than the average startup does at its inception. What you don't—and can't—know at launch, is what relationship this still theoretical business will eventually have to the keystone company. It will take time to know whether an Acorn can live within the keystone forest—whether it will be big enough, have enough momentum, and be strategically relevant. Since there's no way to have these answers at the time of launch, what's most important in positioning the new company is flexibility.

Growing new businesses within or proximate to a larger organization is fundamentally different from building independent external startups. Startups are stand-alones fueled by resources which have no expectation of or interest in owning them. Because eventual ownership is one of a keystone's primary motivations, the Acorn Method's launch strategy is designed to land its new businesses there.

The most likely outcome, of course, as with all new ventures, is that the new company will be shut down at the end of its germination period, if not before. One of the advantages of Acorn businesses, however, is that this outcome isn't nearly as catastrophic as it is for independent companies. The failure of an internal startup doesn't have to be a true failure. Whether an individual Acorn eventually becomes a new high-performing product line or gets shut down, the keystone company will reap significant process benefits and learn a great deal.

Another significant advantage of the Acorn Method is that it provides a third option to the binary of success and failure. While eventual ownership by the keystone is almost always the preferred outcome, in some instances, for any of five reasons which I'll detail in the next chapter, it can be to the keystone's advantage to spin the Acorn *out* rather than in—to establish it as a legally separate, fully independent organization with perhaps a few select people from the keystone on its board but without pre-structured buy-out options and without oversight.

> The success gradient: shut down, spin out, spin in.

Preserving this spin-out option creates a kind of insurance policy for the keystone, allowing it to still capitalize on its investment even if it makes neither strategic nor economic sense to continue owning the new business it grew. The possibility of spinning out can also be an incentive to prospective entrepreneurs as it creates the option of taking ownership themselves and continuing to work on it past the point of the keystone's interest or involvement. It's possible to start a company as a wholly independent entity and to spin it in, but it's difficult to move the other direction—for an Acorn which was germinated as a completely internal project, to move outside the parent organization. Because it's quite possible to lose all these options if they aren't part of your launch strategy, the Acorn Method builds a secure runway at a carefully chosen proximity to its sponsor company.

Launching a new business is an exciting and perilous time. The entrepreneur's usual optimism may grow an edge of anxiety, and the Acorn's primary champion might start to feel out on a limb. To have a runway secure enough to launch, an Acorn needs two things to change: the commitment level and the timeframe.

COMMITMENT

At this point, the commitment of the involved entrepreneurs must change from "Will we?" to "We will." They no longer move on in the face of data that offer anything less than obvious validation. They stop actively seeking reasons to kill the idea and instead dedicate themselves to making it thrive.

The commitment from keystone and/or RES leadership has to change, too. The Acorn has left the corporate branch and should now be treated as an independent entity. As an example, funds should be transferred to a bank account managed solely by the new venture. This is critical because not even the most skillful and experienced entrepreneurs can build a successful new business if, in addition to all the trials of creation, they're fighting to keep the support of the people backing them. Building something from scratch is very different from maintaining or increasing existing growth, and the keystone should recognize that what Acorns need to germinate differs from the internal tools and standard methods it uses to grow and maintain the mother tree, and it must commit to not digging up the new business to see how it's growing.

TIMELINE

When a new business shifts from being grown to needing to grow, the timeline must also change. Acorns germinate more slowly than they fall. The Acorn Method's process phase moved in a series of week- or month-long sprints. This third phase, while still fast-moving, addresses time in longer intervals. Corporations are famously indecisive and the Acorn's entrepreneurial team will want a built-in mechanism to keep things from dragging on indefinitely. At Prehype, we recommend a timeline of eighteen months as the best of several suboptimal triggers. Among the few natural laws of venture businesses, eighteen months to sink or swim is a span everyone can agree on as long enough, but not too long, one which protects everyone both from giving up too easily and from clinging on too long.

Because experiments are, by definition, unpredictable, any other, non-time-based metric or indicator of traction that might be established at the outset is likely to stop being relevant along the way. This leaves both Acorn and keystone without a trigger (with the possible exception of capital) to make a final decision on whether the experiment was a success or failure. While it might seem logical to set a threshold of money spent, doing so creates a counter-productive incentive structure. If the entrepreneurial team knows it will be shut down once it spends a predetermined sum, it may be more motivated to save money than to create a successful business.

Eighteen months is enough time to give seedling businesses every opportunity to succeed, but they can fail much sooner. Sometimes, of course, it becomes clear within the first few months that the seed is a dud—the signal doesn't scale or the opportunity cost for the entrepreneurial team exceeds the value of the opportunity. If there's no reason to wait until the eighteen-month mark, don't.

> Plan on a business-launching runway that's unpredictable, bumpy, and eighteen months long.

PROXIMITY

When an acorn falls from the tree, the biggest question is how far will it go? Too close, and the acorn won't get adequate sun, but acorns carried beyond their parent's habitat are much less likely to survive. As critical as momentum is, it's worth being very strategic about how the keystone and Acorn interact. Perhaps counterintuitively, for the new venture to have the highest probability of success, it needs to germinate somewhere other than where it will eventually take root. There are several reasons for this, but perhaps the most compelling is keeping open the option to spin a successful new business out as well as in.

Regardless of its final destination, the proximity to its parent organization at which a new business can launch ranges from internal project of an existing department to entirely independent new entity. Sometimes, there are practical considerations that make this determination for you. The Acorn company may, for example, depend on access to patents or licenses the keystone holds, or need, for other legal reasons, to be functionally the same company. The right venture structure is tailored to the concept, the keystone, and the team assembled to grow it. Balancing independence and engagement is a delicate and contentious process worth careful consideration because the Acorn's proximity to the keystone will determine the answers to four structural "how" questions:

- How Will It Be Funded?
- How Will It Be Staffed?

- How Will Decisions Be Made?
- How Will Governance and Control Operate?

I'll share some answers to these questions in the Recommendations section that follows, but here, to illustrate the way the range of options relates to the Acorn's distance from its parent organization, I want to imagine a continuum from closest to most distant and give you a snapshot of the way each "how" question operates at either pole.

THE ENTIRELY INTERNAL PROJECT

In this model, funding is allocated to the Acorn through the keystone's innovation department's or the RES's normal budgeting process. Talent is reassigned from within the parent organization and incentivized through its preexisting structure of bonuses or stock options. On a day-to-day basis, there's no discernable difference in the way business is conducted and decisions are made, and there's no legal structure between keystone and Acorn.

THE COMPLETELY NEW ENTITY

Here, the keystone company behaves as if it were making the seed investment in a free-range startup. The Acorn is its own, legally independent new company. It has authority to hire full-time employees to whom it can grant stock or stock options. The Acorn gets very little oversight and doesn't need permission to build, subcontract, or enter into contracts. Governed by its own board from the outset, the only thing that makes this new entity an Acorn business is the keystone company's presence on its board—a presence that does not include a prestructured option to buy out the other shareholders.

THE SPECTRUM

Thinking about this decision as a four-by-four grid helps companies avoid the almost-always fatal mistake of trying to build a chimera—a company for which they contribute minimal funds and over which they exercise maximal control. An Acorn can be located anywhere along the project-entity spectrum, but it cannot be funded as an entity and governed like a project. Keystones should decide where to locate the business(es) they build based on the factors to which they're most sensitive. If, for example, your top priority is running the Acorn as a cheap, scrappy startup motivated by an entrepreneur's sense of ownership and personal investment in the outcome, you must be willing to sacrifice some control over the price of internalizing the company and expanding your forest.

Internal Project ⬅		
FUNDING	• Normal Budgeting Process	• Funded • Fully owned company
TALENT	• Existing employees on direct payroll with stock options and/or bonuses as incentives. • Can be difficult to attract entrepreneurial talent.	• Existing employees and third-party contractors paid on corporate payment terms with custom bonus strategy.
DECISION MAKING	• Standard org chart. • Lots of oversight. • Decisions made slowly.	• Control is budget and management based. • Less Oversight.
GOVERNANCE AND CONTROL	• No separate legal standing follows exiting legal and procurement team rules. • Must request money for each new expenditure. • Able to operate under existing licenses.	• Wholly owned new legal entity. • Assigned a budget, credit card.

Internal Project to New Entity Spectrum

→ **New Entity**

• Shares or convertible loans	• Seed Investors
• Venture teams hired by new company as employees or contractors. • Paid by Paypal. • Often granted stock or stock options.	• Talent employed by new entity. • Easier to attract entrepreneurial types.
• Board-governed by people from the old organization with option under VARIS and IOS to buy out the other shareholders. • Little Oversight.	• Completely Independent, maybe people from old company on board, but no pre-structured buy-out option. • No oversight. • Decisions made quickly.
• Legally independent new company. • Assigned a budget with independent bank accounts.	• Creates and operates own budget. • Must acquire own licenses.

In making decisions about keystone-Acorn proximity, there are five key questions the keystone should consider:

- Is it an absolute must that I be able to buy this company back?
- Do I need this new venture to follow the rules of my legal and procurement teams?
- Am I willing to surrender enough control over the day-to-day decision-making of the Acorn that entrepreneurs will be willing to work there?
- Can this Acorn grow without using our keystone brand?
- Will I be able to keep investing in the continuous growth of this venture after the initial growth phase?

The Original Why

Finally, touching base with the generative problem that sparked the initial idea can help determine at how long an arm's length is appropriate for the existing company to hold the new one.

In the problem-finding process first step (chapter 3) you investigated five opportunity spaces in which to go fishing for interesting problems. As you consider your launch strategy, return to the same point of entry you used which led you to the problem your new venture solves. If your new product or service is a result of having redefined the business you're actually in, you might want more space between it and the existing company. If you developed the new venture in response to customer feedback, it might make sense to start the new business in closer proximity to the old one.

Ranked from closest to most distant, the ordering is typically: responding to customers, anticipating the needs of stakeholders in your space, preemptive disruption, responding to emerging technology or other external changes in the world, and redefining the business you're actually in.

The proximity at which an Acorn is initially established will not be its final location, but it will impact its ultimate relationship to the keystone. In other words, Acorns grown in the canopy can be transplanted. The keystone should establish its new Acorn venture in the position that best addresses the mature company's present priorities and the new one's needs knowing that, in eighteen months or so, they will both be in a much better and more informed position.

RECOMMENDATIONS
PROXIMITY

Spinning the company out is less likely than spinning it in, but can still be a much more profitable outcome than shutting it down, and at the very least a great impetus to the team working on it. To preserve this third option, and to give the new company the best chance of truly taking off, I recommend that during the eighteen-month germination period, the Acorn be situated near the middle of the Internal Project/New Entity continuum.

> Start in the middle and move to the edge.

Here, the new venture operates more independently than it would if it's spun in, but with more oversight than it would be subject to if it's eventually spun out. By initially locating it somewhere near the middle of the continuum between internal project and new entity, you give it both room to stretch its wings and the most solid possible base from which to launch. You also protect the two most important characteristics of a startup organization: speed and flexibility.

Speed

In addition to preserving the option to spin the fledgling company out at the end of its first eighteen months, establishing it at some distance away from the parent allows it to move more quickly on a number of fronts. Decisions can be made more rapidly with fewer people involved, and a shorter feedback loop allows the Acorn to iterate and adjust as it grows.

While commitment, timeline, and keystone-Acorn inter-action change with the shift into the operational phase, it's critical that the startup tempo doesn't slow to keep pace with corporate time. The entrepreneurial team must maintain the same urgency and rigor in workflow with which it worked through the process steps. The timeframe may be longer, measured in months rather than weeks, but the mindset of moving quickly through experimenting and evaluating data, adjusting strategy and tactics, and moving forward must remain the same.

Speed is also a factor in choosing where in the middle to locate the company. In the Internal Project/New Entity Continuum table, column two's big advantage over the otherwise preferable third column is that setting up here is typically a decision the keystone can make very quickly. They already have in place systems for hiring contractors, agencies and other outside organizations that can come in to provide a set of services. Establishing the Acorn under that kind of independent contractor or service agreement allows the keystone to get money into the Acorn and to get it moving quickly.

This is an excellent option for companies that don't already have a system in place for making investments in outside companies. If it would take the keystone a matter of days to get money into an Acorn through a service agreement or six months to buy shares in a new company that it would, in time, come to control, the momentum is worth the cost. In six months, the opportunity will probably be gone.

Flexibility

The entrepreneurial team's mandate isn't to follow the plan with which they launch. Rather, its goal should be less specific: to build a great and successful business for the keystone. To achieve that goal, the team running an inside startup needs the flexibility to pivot and take the company in new directions as it evolves and new opportunities arise. Having some distance from the larger, more stable company allows for greater flexibility.

> Your job is to build the best business, not to follow the plan.

In addition to protecting the spin-out option and persevering the entrepreneurial pace and flexibility, positioning the Acorn company midway between the project/entity poles shapes my recommendations for how to answer the four "how" questions I posed above.

HOW WILL IT BE FUNDED?

Because it's critical to keep up the project's momentum,

entrepreneurial teams should have quite a lot of leeway in how money is spent. Having to submit a request form each time they need to make a hire or purchase will slow them down, a drag which can be very costly in terms of the project's odds of success.

Like the acorn, which needs to sustain the growth of its root system for months on stored energy before it's capable of photosynthesis, I strongly recommend the new venture have ready access to an adequate reserve of cash. This can be as simple as setting it up with a credit card or separate bank account, and will allow the new company to:

- Hire a full-time employee without going through the keystone's HR process
- Hire a contractor without having to bid out the contract through the sometimes arcane operating procedures of the keystone's purchasing department
- Bring in a freelancer for a few hours of work and pay them without the ninety-day delay the keystone's normal terms require

Additionally, the success of an entrepreneurial team depends on its ability to devise experiments, run them, recalibrate, and retest in rapid cycles. Needing to justify each experiment to managers unfamiliar with this kind of operation grinds progress to a standstill. Team leaders become distracted from their real work of validating their assumptions about the company's viability by the need to justify their process or manage internal politics. It's possible for the senior leadership of keystone organizations to be unfamiliar with, if not overtly hostile to, the startup culture's relatively free-form (or lack of) structure. The method is appropriate to the material, and has repeatedly been proven successful, but it is different. And different isn't always warmly embraced.

I believe it is precisely this discomfort with an unfamiliar process rather than the uncertainty about its ultimate profitability that causes the most conflict. I've seen companies that balk at investing in Acorn enterprises be completely willing to spend heavily on a marketing event that everyone acknowledges will be pure cost, simply because such spending doesn't feel experimental.

HOW WILL IT BE STAFFED?

To a certain extent, each Acorn business is a microcosm of the keystone company. The five or so people running it will need to perform all the functions the five thousand employees of the larger one do, on a shorter timeline and with a commitment to ongoing experimentation, so it's critical to get the right people on board.

> Generally speaking, the more distance an Acorn has from the keystone company, the more able it will be to attract strong entrepreneurial talent.

Entrepreneurs are more likely to be turned off by close links to a long-established and successful company than they are to be attracted to its reputation and stability. The personalities that are successful in these positions want to take a risk on something cutting edge much more than they want a staff pass and a pension, and they'll expect an incentive structure that isn't a direct correlation to any already in place at the keystone.

Most entrepreneurial types are more accustomed to and more interested in owning equity or equity-like interests than in being compensated in a more traditional format. They're motivated by a desire to build something of value and importance, but they also want their remuneration to reflect the opportunity costs they incur by dedicating a year or more of their professional lives to gambling on it. Finally, it can be an inducement to entrepreneurs to know that, if the keystone ends up cutting off its investments in the new company, that the entrepreneur will have options to continue it on their own.

Not surprisingly, we strongly recommend recruiting, compensating, and incentivizing the highest caliber minds you can bring onboard. Finding talent that's right for this type of project is obviously extremely difficult. My favorite shortcut is similar to the one I recommended for identifying the right people to enlist in problem finding. Ask yourself: "Who, in my industry, is most likely to leave within a few years to found a startup?" Beyond that simple barometer, I've found that the people who tend to be most successful on Acorn teams tend to share some or all of the following traits:

① **A rebel identity.** They're people who look at challenges from multiple, sometimes idiosyncratic perspectives which can seem contrarian, if not downright antagonistic, to stability and repeatability. They don't just ponder what to do, but how to do it.

② **The art of selling the future.** They're conceptual thinkers with a gift for expressing abstract ideas and unproven theories in ways that excite others. They can sell the present on the future and get people to fall in love with things that don't yet exist. They understand that emotions drive sales and are willing to take emotional responsibility for new ideas.

③ **Impact over credit.** They find fulfillment in completion more than in the approval of others, and would rather make a difference than a name for themselves.

④ **Scrappiness.** These people aren't delicate. They get

things done without enough time, people, or money. They know how to reduce the risk of failure by reducing the cost of trying, and they're not afraid to try.

⑤ **The beauty of the fringe.** They're curious about skills that aren't their forte and in areas of expertise not their own, and they're constantly prowling all those edges as well as the boundaries of their organization, their value chain and their process for ways to make new things happen.

⑥ **Action over analysis.** These people have a bias toward action and an experimental mindset. They tinker and tweak, experiment and play. They always seem a bit impatient.

It fascinates me that the best such people rarely have the shiniest resumes. The most talented entrepreneurs I've recruited have been everything from failed founders to toy designers to professional jazz trombonists.

HOW WILL DECISIONS BE MADE?

Prehype has helped establish entrepreneurial ventures within organizations so large that it could take weeks to get on the calendar of someone in the finance or tech team. The legal team could take even longer to return a decision. This careful, custodial pace will kill a new

Acorn venture which can only move forward as quickly as decisions are made. It's important for the entrepreneurs running an Acorn to have access to the institutional wisdom of the keystone, but they need to not feel constrained by it. Acorns must be able to make their own decisions quickly.

HOW WILL GOVERNANCE AND CONTROL OPERATE?

An Acorn, like most startups, needs a board, and I recommend that it include, in addition to the Acorn's lead entrepreneur or founder, two or three key stakeholders from the RES or and/or keystone. Typically, this should be the Chief Innovation Officer and, depending on the needs of both keystone and Acorn, a person from legal, finance, and/or marketing. Ideally, you want to include the keystone people in whom a sense of ownership will be most beneficial to the Acorn's future, and who are also future-oriented and idealistic enough to keep the Acorn's growth from being encumbered by a myopic (or even cynical) over-focus on detail and procedure.

> To allow for meaningful, consistent, engaged conversation, limit your board to not more than five people.

Make it clear that these two or three people from the

keystone are now the ones designated to get updates and disseminate relevant information to appropriate parties within the larger organization. This protects the Acorn from all the other interested people who might otherwise pick up the phone or pop by the office with questions (and worse, suggestions) which will pull the entrepreneurs' focus and may put the entire endeavor off course or behind schedule.

It's also a very good idea to include someone from outside the keystone who is not otherwise involved in the new venture, but in whose authority as an entrepreneur the organization puts a good deal of confidence and trust. This is most often an external advisor, hired by the company, who's able to speak on behalf of the entrepreneur. This person serves as both translator and arbiter, able to balance the keystone's need for what is familiar and comprehensible with the Acorn's tendency toward non-conformity if not down-right rebellion.

This advisor is charged with telling the truth to power and talking sense to innovation. He or she is responsible for providing the needed perspective both when the founders insist even the most obvious portents of failure can be overcome, and when the keystone is underwhelmed by a six-month return of $30,000 as a fraction of what they do in sales, despite it being a remarkably good number for the startup.

Cadence of an Acorn Board

At intervals no shorter than three weeks, the Acorn's lead entrepreneur should report back to the board on the new company's overall trajectory—the direction it's headed, and how quickly it's getting there. I've found that a combination of written and in-person reporting works best with monthly updates from the founder, and a meeting of the board once a quarter.

Keeping key members of the sponsor company updated on a reliable schedule avoids a great deal of the weird behavior that can happen when there isn't a prescribed way of getting questions answers and anxieties allayed. The keystone is able to reassure itself that the Acorn is operating within the canopy and not doing anything out of bounds. It's also an opportunity for the Acorn's learnings to be transferred to the larger organization.

Benefits of a Board

Any entrepreneur with a startup knows they need to service the relationship they have with their investors. Experienced entrepreneurs will also recognize the benefits of a system which requires them to occasionally get enough distance from their immediate work to take the long view of their collective activity. A commitment to monthly written reports to the board form the basis of an excellent practice of regular check-ins with the Acorn's broader vision, with how it's tracking against its North Star, and with how much it has changed and progressed in a single month.

> Monthly reporting is as necessary to the venture as it is to the sponsor. Probably more.

A founder can easily spend all day every day up at HQ providing updates to the fifty different stakeholders who think they have a reason for interest in the Acorn's business. The board becomes a shield enabling the entrepreneur to politely refer all distractions and inquiries back to the people on the board with a simple appeal to protocol.

Founders should also see these regular touch points as a sales opportunity of sorts that keep upper management excited about the project. Since it depends entirely on funds from the keystone, keeping the decision-makers at the sponsoring company energized and excited about the project works to everyone's benefit. The early data coming out of an Acorn is rarely so empirically promising that people can see, from a written update in spreadsheet or report form that there's cause for optimism. The chance to explain the data in its best, most promising and inspiring light, and to remind key stakeholders that a talented team of people are working hard and hitting milestones, can make the difference between an Acorn that succeeds and one that's shut down prematurely.

IDENTITY

While most of my recommendations for building an Acorn's secure runway at a carefully chosen proximity to its sponsor company have been influenced by that proximity, I have a less nuanced recommendation about the Acorn's identity. An Acorn should not operate under the keystone's brand. It should have, at minimum, a new corporate identity with a different name, logo, email addresses, and website. This can seem counterintuitive to the keystone who sees their brand as an asset that would work in the Acorn's favor both in terms of name recognition and trust, but those advantages are outweighed by those of forging a new corporate identity.

> Give the new venture a new identity.

Nike, for example, when it launched Easy Kicks, set the new enterprise up outside its corporate campus, deliberately creating perceived and physical distance between oak and Acorn. Easy Kicks, then, interacted with the public and with other companies as if it were an entirely new and unrelated startup venture. They gave up Nike's name recognition and reputation for quality in order to benefit from the predisposition people have to cheer on young upstarts. Suppliers are more likely to make concessions on price for a new business, and early adopters are more interested in backing the indie than the corporate.

There are pros and cons of creating physical distance between the old and new companies, and we've seen both be successful. A separate location can make it easier for a new project team to establish its own culture, but such an arrangement sacrifices the ability to maintain a casual interface between the two companies, and can create a kind of innovation island which might be out of sight and out of mind.

CHAPTER SUMMARY

For the keystone organization that has grown an Acorn either as a one-off or within an RES, the shift from idea to action can be a formidable one. As a new venture moves out into the world to start solving the problem you identified for an increasing number of people, managing the relationship between it and the keystone organization requires a strategy that can manage all three possible outcomes: shut down, spin out, and spin in. The commitment and timelines change and more distance is created to allow the Acorn to grow a startup speed. You need strategies to handle funding and governance and control, and new talent needs to be brought into the organization.

Once the structural and brand distances from the keystone are established and a mechanism is in place for communication between the two, the work of starting an Acorn business is not substantively different from a startup grown in the wild. It's beyond the Acorn Method's scope to go through the virtues and operation of web analytics and knowing when and how to pivot, but there are many resources available on how to run a startup, and Appendix A includes a list of titles I think are particularly good. There are, however, several considerations unique to an Acorn as it starts down the eighteen-month runway, and one very unique outcome that we'll discuss in the next chapter.

CHAPTER 8

...

Launch Your Business

Having executed on the strategy of building a secure runway at a carefully chosen proximity from the keystone or RES, you're ready to take the Acorn Method's final strategic step—launching your new business! Whether created within a larger company or, if the Acorn Method's Structure has been implemented, within an RES, your Acorn business is ready to taxi down its eighteen-month runway to lift-off. This final strategy covers that run, what to do if the launch fails, and how to fly.

RUN

The experience of the shift from securing and situating a runway to actually running down it is well summarized by the great philosopher, Mike Tyson: "Everyone has a plan until they get punched in the face." Typically, the first day of operations—the day you stop selling an idea to upper management and start selling a product to clients—is that day. You get punched in the face and toss out your plans. The Acorn Method has a two R's and three S's strategy to leave you in a better position (by which I mean still punching back) than odds would otherwise suggest at the end of your eighteen-month runway. These are: reporting, revenue, speed, spending, and sales.

During the germination period, founders of Acorn companies are in a position similar to, but not quite the same as, any other entrepreneur with a new startup. Certainly, you still want to follow the best practices found in any good book on startup thinking—being experimental, having KPIs or OKRs against which to meticulously measure progress, designing thoughtful experiments to test the fitness of your model, and investing more in those that work. Treating the first eighteen months of an Acorn's life as a collection of experiments is the only way to build the momentum your new venture will need to survive even that long. Establish a framework for aggressively forming hypotheses about different parts of your business and create tools to implement ways of testing those hypotheses. Measure the results and very dispassionately determine where you were right, where you were wrong, and what to do next.

Unlike the typical startup, however, an Acorn company

will be reporting to its keystone or RES rather a VC firm or other investors, and therefore it needs to manage both its reporting and its metrics somewhat differently.

REPORTING

In the last chapter, I recommended a cadence of monthly reporting to keep your keystone or RES updated on the Acorn's growth, but these monthly reports have value all on their own. I've noticed a stronger (at least anecdotal) correlation between a new business's success and some form of monthly reporting than perhaps any other factor. I think this has less to do with the positive impact of those reports on securing the startup's source of funds, than with the simple discipline of having regular checkpoints. It probably wouldn't matter if no one else saw the output if, without the pressure of external expectations, founders were able to make themselves stop and go through the process of reflection, recalibration, and recommitment. It's an incredibly powerful exercise to plan based on what key results you want to be able to report to your board in your next monthly report. Think about the report you want to write at the end of next month and design this month's experiments to get you there.

REVENUE

Because an Acorn lives from monthly update to monthly

update, you specifically need to measure those precursors of growth your keystone or RES will most readily understand and find exciting. I recommend making money. Revenue, the second R of the Acorn Method's 2R 3S strategy, is a bit of a blunt object, but still one of the best ways to gauge whether people are responding positively to the product or service you're offering to solve one of their problems, and it's a happy medium between absolute, empirical cash flow (on which mature businesses are valued), and arbitrary, conceptual growth indicators like Facebook likes.

The Venture Capital community typically solves for growth above all else on the thesis that growth eventually translates into revenue, and such investors are often willing to invest in new markets, confident they'll be able to monetize them later. In that environment, new users, industry buzz, and lines of new code written can be a perfectly valid, even exciting metrics. VC investors are frequently happy to funnel money into moonshots that, in the unlikely event of success, could be truly revolutionary. Keystone companies, however, tend to be much more focused on terrestrial targets. There's less leeway in the interpretation of what counts as a precursor to value in these situations, and an Acorn needs to speak the language which its RES or keystone—its only investor—understands most readily.

Measure success by revenue.

Revenue is simply more important to a keystone or RES-grown startup than to one created anywhere else. No early-stage business is expected to generate a lot in true cash flow or profits—it needs to be aggressively reinvesting in its own growth—but the ability to demonstrate that money is actually coming in is more likely than anything else to encourage the keystone to keep up its investment. How much money you bring in and how quickly that number grows is the most compelling argument your Acorn can make for its continued survival. You are very literally buying time. My metric hierarchy is: cash first, cash second, with the acquisition of new customers previously beyond the keystone's reach in third place.

SPEED

A monthly reporting rhythm only gives you enough time to accomplish things if you keep up the pressure to move extremely quickly. And you must. Eighteen months will go by much faster than you'd care to imagine! Every decision you make should be weighed against its ability to spur or hobble forward momentum. Almost everything you're creating in these early months is going to be replaced eventually, so right now, done really is better than art.

> Solve for speed, and trust the result will be positive business outcomes.

If it takes two weeks to find and commission the ideal graphic designer to work on your logo, grab a good-enough designer who can get it done tomorrow. You can redo it if you want to once you're huge. Don't think about the work you're doing in these eighteen months as laying a foundation that will need to support the full weight of all your ambition. A new venture isn't a building, it's an Acorn. Grow it into a tree quickly or the squirrels will eat it. If it survives, there will be time later to prune it into a more attractive shape.

SPENDING

Spending is the second S in the Acorn Method's 2R 3S Strategy, and since the two most valuable assets you have in building a successful new business (or in life) are time and money, I want to give you a few recommendations on how to best spend each.

Money

Your capital burn rate is my one exception to the faster-is-better rule. Move quickly simply for the sake of moving quickly, but save money for the sake of extending your runway. If your keystone or RES has given you eighteen months of capital, plan to make it last for thirty-six. Don't fall victim to the linear spending model in which you take eighteen months of money and distribute it evenly over eighteen months. If you want to divvy it up, reserve half for spending in the final month. At this stage, burn time, conserve cash.

If, at the end of your first six months, you've done nine months of work but spent two months' money, not only will you have bent the curve on what you have left, you'll be in a position to make smarter, more informed decisions about how to spend the remaining sixteen months' worth of funds. You'll be able to put it where it will be most valuable to you, which is a great position to be in with a year left in which to prove yourselves.

Time

Because you have so little and it moves so quickly, you must be rigorous in prioritizing how you spend your time. I have a simple rule of thumb: the next right thing to undertake is almost always the one that makes you most uncomfortable. Spending your Acorn's first months finding cool desks, hiring great people and going to conferences does not pass this test. That would be fun and will leave you with a cool office, a brilliant team, and no business.

> Save money, especially on things that create more ambiance than income.

Hiring people may be the most seductive fun a founder can have—even more than deciding between elaborate coffee machines. I get it. Starting a new business is lonely and hiring lets you see your enthusiasm reflected in people who, very flatteringly, want to be a part of what you're doing. Working for a startup is exciting. People will like your ideas and people always like money. Hiring them is exhilarating for everyone. So obviously, it fails the discomfort test.

Instead, you need to be like the circus clown who dashes back and forth to keep the spinning plates balanced on their sticks, touching each one the moment before it topples, and just enough to keep it aloft. Do most of the jobs in the company yourself, at least initially, and then hire people—not fill a position, but to perform a function that solves whatever is causing the greatest drag on your time. In other words, hire to increase your speed, not to fill an org chart. Like all other planning documents, expect that one not to survive contact with reality. If you wait, you'll discover you don't actually need many of those positions at all, much less as early hires. You won't know which positions are truly necessary until you see where the absence of a person executing in that space is slowing you down.

> Often, the only way you'll know what to hire people to do is by having done it yourself.

Worse, when you hire someone without a specific mandate, one of two things happen: One, nothing. Two, they make something up. If you've hired talented people they'll probably do a fine job of assigning themselves work and completing it, but the best results come from tasking such talent with optimizing rather than inventing the work their positions entail. To know what that is, you need to have done it.

Hiring too early is rooted in the fallacy that a startup should be future-ready. It's very easy to start thinking too far ahead, especially with the primacy I've encouraged you to place on speed. Being slow to spend money and prioritizing time on the uncomfortable helps downshift in the right places, and hiring is one of those places.

Back in the early days of BarkBox, when people heard my co-founders and I were packing the boxes ourselves, everyone was very quick to point out that this practice wouldn't scale. That was true, but not a problem. Preparation is a luxury. Solve today's problems today because if you don't, you'll never get to the ones you prepared for. The first problem for BarkBox, as for all new ventures, was getting customers. We didn't need a system for packing boxes we hadn't sold. We needed to sell boxes.

My wife, Mette, helping me pack boxes in the early days of BarkBox.

By the time we'd sold enough boxes to be slowed down by packing them ourselves, we'd learned what the process required and were able to hand over a system to people we hired to execute and improve upon. There's an enormous difference between bringing people on board to do a job you've been doing (and charging them with finding ways to do it faster, better, and more efficiently) and hiring people to figure out what needs to be done and how to do it for the first time. Don't hire someone until you know specifically what you're hiring them to do, then let them optimize the process. Solve for What. Hire for How.

These are very different skills. One's not intrinsically better than the other, and a company won't survive without both, but typically, the ability to invent and to replicate, to establish and to maintain aren't present to the same degree in one person. Play to your strengths as a one-and-done or repeat-and-refine person and hire for the other skillset.

> People who excel at getting something off the ground are often poor pilots.

In an Acorn's early days, its entire complement of three or four people should each expect to do a hundred different jobs. As a company grows, it will need fewer multi-function people and more specialized expertise. This can create tension between those who were best suited to positions that are no longer necessary, but without which the new jobs wouldn't exist, and those brought in later to do those jobs.

SALES

If hiring is some of the most fun an entrepreneur can have, selling may be one of the most uncomfortable. If you're ever wondering what you should be doing with your time, selling something is never the wrong answer. In fact, in the first six months, it's almost always the best answer. Sales is the 2R 3S Strategy's final "S" not just because revenue is an Acorn's best metric of success. If the core activities of business-building are fundraising, hiring, building a product, and selling it, selling is the most information-creating activity and, especially in the first six months, you must be an information-seeking organism. The work of the eighteen-month runway is experimentation, and if revenue is the desired outcome, all the experiments you run are sales experiments; cash is feedback.

> You will live and die by your feedback loops. Complete as many as possible.

Another advantage of moving quickly and spending slowly is that it allows you to complete the maximum number of feedback loops. This increases the odds that one experiment or an aggregate of several will return the critical information or prompt the crucial pivot that turns a good idea into a terrific product—and your Acorn into a tree.

Design all your experiments to return feedback in one of two forms—cash (preferably) and information. Feedback in the form of money increases both revenue, which improves your overall odds of success, and the number of feedback loops you're able to perform. Finally, sales aren't just the most desirable form of feedback, they're also the highest quality. For all the reasons we discussed in chapter 6, people are most honest when their money is on the line. There are a hundred reasons people will tell you something about your product or service, there's only one reason they'll pay you for it—you've made something they want at a price they deem reasonable.

> Move fast, spend slow, and sell stuff.

Design your sales experiments to test this hypothesis: "I think you, potential customer, have a particular problem, and that our product or service will solve it at a price you're willing to pay." Your hypothesis is correct to the extent that the right customers pay the right price for the right solution to the right problem. If your product or service isn't all four kinds of right, your hypothesis is wrong. Your experiment, however, is still a success if it delivers information about which or what combination of those targets you missed in the form of actionable feedback.

Act on actionable feedback. Responding to feedback by

revising or redesigning or even redirecting, and then heading back into the feedback-seeking (selling) process again, keeps building success on success. An experiment is a success if it returns feedback in either spendable or actionable form, and a transcendent success if it brings in both. If people indicate their agreement with your hypothesis by paying you for it and then subsequently recommend it to their friends who also vote yes with cash, you've found not just a good solution to a felt problem, but a magnetic solution to a shared problem.

FAILURE TO LAUNCH

By the time you've gotten an Acorn on the runway, you've already invested a great deal of time, energy, and emotion. There's a tremendous amount of inertia to overcome, particularly inside a big organization, to get anything approved, much less actually revved up and underway. If you work through the Process steps, build a secure runway and deflect a punch or two with your strategic two R's and three S's, only to discover that everything you've gotten the keystone to buy into is wrong, it's almost too exhausting to think about going back and doing it again. Not wanting to face the pain of failure, you'll be tempted to sink more money, energy, and time into postponing it.

If you find yourself blaming the customer for not understanding your solution or accusing marketing of not doing its job, odds are, your Acorn is dead. Time to call it and move on. Remember, the experiments you're conducting are experiments. You're searching for signs of life. If you don't find them, it's probably not because you haven't looked hard or long enough or in the right place with the right gear, it's because there's no life to find.

Simply having made it onto the runway meant that you'd developed a solution that actively attracted customers that you had good reasons to be optimistic. There's a kind of natural selection that almost guarantees optimism as a character attribute of anyone who sets out to make something from nothing. It's an admirable survival trait but one which, combined with a very human aversion to pain, can lead entrepreneurs across the boundary from courage into deliberate blindness. Stopping the wrong idea is sometimes harder than starting the right one. Most new ventures fail, and often a quick death is the best bad answer. You have to be prepared to kill stuff.

Failure hurts. To compensate for this truth and the truth of its inevitability, there's a lie some entrepreneurs tell themselves about the glory of failure. I don't think anybody should celebrate failure. Nobody wants to fail. Instead, accept failure as inevitable, and do what you can to both reduce its cost and extract from it all the value it holds.

Failure may feel like death, but it isn't. Let me reassure

you—if you ran a series of experiments that failed, but you created a lot of learning, tried interesting things, and worked hard and with integrity—your project may be dead, but your career isn't even wounded. I've never seen an honorable failure have a negative impact on a person's career as long as they didn't let it cripple their spirit. Rather than buy into the modern, Silicon Valley fetishization of failure, I recommend the medieval *memento mori* model and practice the Default Death stance I recommended in Signal Mining: Expect to kill a project unless the data scream at you not to.

> Failure is inevitable, painful, and not as damaging for your career as you're afraid it is.

As was also the case in Signal Mining, the obvious failures are easier than the edge cases, but with more time and heart invested at this point, I want to give you a more nuanced model for how to know when your new venture won't fly. It's a model that learns from science and with love.

SCIENCE

Scientists don't try to prove a hypothesis; they actively seek to disprove it. In fact, the closest they can get to proof is the absence of disproof. To be valid, a scientific trial needs to be double-blind and conducted by an impartial, unvested third party. In science, a hypothesis based on observed data is considered untrue until it amasses enough evidence to be deemed a viable theory. In entrepreneurship, and Acorns, we take almost the opposite approach, we come up with an idea we like and undertake to prove it's the right solution to a problem we also largely invented. But if we didn't, startups would be as rare as scientific certainty.

LOVE

The other, contrasting model to science's hypothesis-and-experiment is the plunge-and-paddle of romance. As entrepreneurs, we fall in love with an idea and strive to keep it afloat sometimes past the point where it's dragging us under. In entrepreneurship, as in love, popular wisdom advises ignoring solid evidence and "working on" the relationship. This is often excellent advice. Relationships and businesses are hard and require effort, commitment, and the investment of time and passion. But we've all seen friends stay past the point of reason and miss a chance at something better because it's just too excruciating to leave.

LIFE

The virtue of the default death model is that, particularly

in the Process phase, it conserves your energy for those projects with the best chance at survival. The two other models, science plus love, equal life. Take the plunge but don't lose your head. Look for evidence of success rather than of failure, but insist that evidence match your strength of feeling. It's "hell yes or no." Only a few of the projects I've worked on were a sure thing from the first date, but all the eventual winners began to generate energy pretty quickly. I married my wife because just reading the papers together on a Sunday morning is exciting to me.

Energy is life. When you're trying to create something from nothing, you put energy into an idea—a lifeless thing. If you get energy back, congratulations, Dr. Frankenstein! An oak tree produces 10,000 acorns for each one that results in an eventual tree, and while the odds for a new business are better than that, most ideas stay in the realm of thought and not survive the transition into the world of living things. Put your energy into people and projects, and where you get energy back, throw everything you've got at it because it's rare. The default is always death.

FLY!

Many new ventures don't make it to the end of their eighteen-month runway, but where, at the end of this period, your Acorn shows strong signs of life, it's time to set a destination. You need to be disciplined about this process as momentum is still critical, but finding the best new location for a thriving new business follows a three-stop shopping process of determining where its value is. I touched on some possible destinations in the previous chapter, but the complete list, in order of preference, is: transplant the Acorn into the keystone forest, transplant it out, or, in rare instances, extend its germination for another three to eighteen months.

TRANSPLANT IN

In this, the most desirable scenario, the Acorn has value because someone inside the keystone organization thinks it does. Typically, this value is realized in one of two ways: acquisition or reverse merger. In each, use of the verb, "buy" is italicized to indicate these transactions are rarely true purchases, but transfers of assets and liabilities.

Acquisition

The Acorn is valuable to the keystone in and of itself, and is *bought* by the keystone's Mergers and Acquisitions team which then integrates it through their established process.

Reverse Merger

The Acorn, while having not necessarily created a viable

new line of business for the keystone, is valuable for its ability to reinvigorate an existing one. Here, the Acorn *buys* a keystone stagnant product line related or similar to its new product or service within the keystone transplanting in the startup's vitality and fresh DNA.

This arrangement is appealing to the Acorn team because it gives them a much larger base from which to execute their vision, and it benefits the keystone by grafting the velocity of the new to the mass of the old. The momentum compounds under new leadership, with a new brand, a reenergized strategic direction, fresh insights and an updated thought process about who the line's customers are and what they want.

TRANSPLANT OUT

Sometimes, at the end of the eighteen months, an Acorn has grown into what the keystone recognizes as a great business which isn't for them. Either it doesn't fit with the overall strategy of the organization, or the Acorn, in the course of its growth, pivoted into a space that's distant enough from the keystone's core business that it no longer makes sense to own it; they'd rather convert their investment and become a minority equity holder.

There are three other more unusual circumstances in which it makes sense to spin an Acorn out:

- It's strategically relevant, but the capital required to achieve its mandate is more than the keystone has the appetite to fund. Acorn is spun out to bring in external investors.
- The keystone wants to be a customer or client of an Acorn's new product or service which needs to be democratized to be useful. Other players in the same industry need to create a consortium of users for the Acorn to fulfill its value proposition.
- The keystone believes the Acorn is failing and is no longer willing to continue funding it, but the entrepreneurial team has a more optimistic view or a higher tolerance for uncertainty. Here, there's really no cost to the keystone to spin the Acorn out, take their share in it, and allow the entrepreneurs to do what they can. If the entrepreneurs can't make it work, the keystone is in exactly the same position it would have been had it shut the venture down. Sometimes, however, such an Acorn, after finding third parties (other corporate or financial partners) to fund a longer runway, eventually takes off. Having taken on no more additional risk, the keystone ends up owning a minority share in a company whose entrepreneurial team managed to turn into a silk purse.

REMAIN IN PLACE

Very occasionally, there's an argument for choosing to

invest more in the status quo. If a late pivot shows strong possibilities but hasn't had enough time to prove itself, or if some aspect of product development was unexpectedly complex, the keystone or RES may let the existing dynamic play out over an additional six to twelve months. They'll need to recalibrate how much capital goes in, and to reset what the options at the end of the extended runway will be. I'd strongly caution anyone—keystone, RES, or Acorn—to be wary of the sunk cost fallacy here. Don't waste resources tending a frail offshoot any longer than a total of three years.

CHAPTER SUMMARY

Having gone operational, an Acorn needs a solid strategy for managing its bumpy and unpredictable trek down the runway as it (hopefully) takes off. The Acorn Method's second strategy consists of the two R's and three S's of revenue, reporting, speed, spending, and sales. Make revenue your primary indicator of progress, report on that progress monthly, and move as quickly as possible. Spend money sparingly, particularly in the early months, and prioritize selling over any other use of your time.

Whether you've implemented all eight steps of the Acorn Method, established an RES within your keystone organization and handed its operation off to a Studio Lead, or were, yourself, involved only in the four creation steps and two growth strategies, shutting down, spinning in or spinning out a new Acorn business wraps up the sequence. Please don't let it describe the limits of your business forest. A single tree has a life cycle, but a forest is a cycle of cycles. A tree generates an acorn, an acorn generates another tree, and the forest regenerates itself expanding to incorporate new products and reach new markets. It renews itself by creating new entities in exciting, expanding regenerative growth rings.

CHAPTER 9

• • •

Notes from the Air

Because I've been an independent and an Acorn entrepreneur and am still connected to both worlds, I often advise people who are starting the bold work of building a new organization. Over the years, the advice I most frequently give has distilled itself into recommendations that I'll pass on here. I imagine you now, not reading, but sitting across a beer from me saying, "Hey, I think I'm going to start building a business inside a business. What can you tell me that I don't already know?"

I don't know how you decided to create something from nothing. Maybe you were tasked with it. Maybe you put your hand up when asked to take it on. Maybe you're the rebel insider who's going to build a business inside your organization without its prior blessing. You might be heading up an Acorn team or leading a new Revenue Exploration Studio. It doesn't really matter how you got here with me enjoying our beers. Every origin story is unique, but they all share a set of defining features, and my advice covers those.

LAUNCH SOMETHING

At the outset, because they're all (basically) rational people, an organization's leadership will probably acknowledge that building a new business inside their company is going to be difficult. They'll recognize such ventures take time and cost money. You and everyone involved will agree on what appears to be a perhaps aggressive, but sane timeline.

But Acorns are interesting and people get curious. Before you're ready, someone, usually from the CFO's office, will start wondering what you've done to yield results. If the only thing you've accomplished is getting a cool office set up, no one is going to be impressed, not even by your color-coordinated foosball table. You're then going to be put under a disproportionate amount of extra pressure to create some kind of result to justify yourself. This will not make your already difficult work any easier. Even if you've been told you have three years, and they've put it in the budget, and they swear they understand the vagaries of this kind of work, I can promise you, you will start to see people showing up and asking for results quicker than they promised. Plan for the keystone's patience to run out well before they anticipated.

> Expect everything to take longer than you expect.

I've stressed the importance of momentum and moving quickly throughout this book, but nowhere is it more critical than in your first few months of runway. From the first day, get going on the job of building something you can launch as quickly as you possibly can, ideally by the ninety-day mark.

DOCUMENT EVERYTHING

One of the steepest challenges an Acorn team faces is the need to justify its existence. The difficulty of setting goals and establishing KPIs for something that inherently is—and should be—uncertain, only this is harder. The closest thing I have to a silver bullet is to document your experiments. If you're designing them properly, every experiment will teach you something. Capture those learnings and package them in a form you are then able to share with the whole keystone or RES. Helping others prevent a mistake you've made generates value and demonstrates a return on investment.

> Documentation is a product you can ship.

Establish this habit from the very beginning. The best

insurance you can have in a business as uncertain as building businesses may be the ability to say: "We have done the following experiments, and while they have not yielded a new, successful business, we have learned a number of useful things which are now available to the rest of the organization in an easily accessible package."

Keep this documentation short, simple and easy to consume. For each experiment, give a brief description, the expected outcome, the actual outcome, and what would be required for someone else to replicate the experiment. Leverage your relationship with the keystone to get this distributed. If, for example, you came up with a cool new way of emailing customers that didn't really do much for your Acorn, but could be usefully deployed across the keystone's larger sales and marketing efforts, it could yield a high return on the company's investment and would be a success regardless of the new venture's final fate.

TELL THE HAPPIEST TRUTH

In the face of resistance, inertia and disinterest, if you're running an RES or Acorn, it's your job to keep the energy up and to sell the decision-makers in the keystone, the talent you want to recruit, and the people at home who love you on the wisdom of taking this particular leap. Inertia will work against you as will a nearly universal institutional preference for keeping its feet on the ground. The default position, especially inside large organizations is to deny almost every nonstandard request.

When you need the okay of a large committee and one "no" vote can shut you down, you'll want to make yes-winning promises. When you're trying to convince a hot new talent to come and work with you, and they're resistant because you're not a sexy lean startup, you may tempt them options you swear will be worth a lot before long. You'll tell your family that this time will be different (just like you do every time). You'll promise your investors that this is going to be huge.

You'll stand up and cheerlead, then you'll sit alone and panic. That's your job.

You're the confidence bearer and the idea monger. You signed up to take onto your own shoulders the anxiety for the risks you're urging on everyone else. Don't expect reassurance from anyone, but don't hide discouraging data.

Since positivity is part of your job, it can be tempting to downplay bad news or fudge what the odds are. Don't do it. Bring the direct and indirect stakeholders along for the journey, and be transparent with them about the challenges you confront. Secrecy will only blow up in your face. Remind stakeholders that what you're attempting is difficult and that failure is possible, even probable. Remind them that an educational failure is still a good outcome. When you share the obstacles you're facing with stakeholders, share your plan for addressing them. They'll appreciate the transparency and may even be able to clear a few roadblocks for you.

STAND OUT, DON'T FIT IN

Resist the temptation to integrate too easily with the keystone. Don't build your Acorn in the image of the oak. Your value to the larger organization lies in your differences, not your similarities. Don't get dragged into a discussion about those metrics by which established businesses are measured but which don't apply to you. For example, an Acorn should track top line growth, not profits; and since its scale is smaller, its profit margins won't be as wide. You're not a large company, don't let yourself be measured like one. Conversely, don't look to the startup world for your comparisons. Corporate ventures have many more constraints, and are often billed differently.

Likewise, be very selective about which of the keystone's resources you use. If you avail yourself of existing HR infrastructure, for example, you'll likely only reach the same talent pool the keystone's already fished. You don't have to reinvent everything, but look critically at hand-me-down norms.

This may make you unpopular. Don't care. There will likely be jealousies within the keystone organization—people who resent the funding you get and the fun you're having. As long as the senior stakeholder is on board, it really doesn't matter that there are people in core conversations gunning for you. Doing things differently and doing different things is inherently annoying to some people. Annoy them.

Expect not to have a lot of friends at the keystone and plan to be okay with it. Don't spend much time defending what you're doing. If possible, find a way of distancing your project from the organization enough that your presence isn't a constant invitation to take potshots at you. But do this only if it doesn't compromise your ability to stay close—physically close—to your sponsor. You don't have to be on the same floor as your inside advocate, but create a space that's easy for him or her swing by. You want to carefully nurture your relationship with such people and make sure they feel involved, maintain buy-in, and see everything that's going on.

SEEK EXPERIENCE

I've said previously anyone who solves problems in a

scalable way is an entrepreneur, and I deeply believe this to be true. It's also a bit like saying anyone who jogs is a runner. While that may be the case, not every runner should take on a marathon. The skillset of actually building a business from scratch goes beyond being entrepreneurial. Entrepreneurship is a mindset, and it's a great place to start, but there's a difference between having tried to build a company before, and being a smart person who's intrigued and creative and interested in the space. Enjoy both, but hire experience. You'd probably be better served by bringing in the guy who started his own mobile pet grooming business than staffing your Acorn team with your ad agency, even if it's full of smart, creative people who think it sounds really cool to build a new business with you.

Hire experience, but befriend it as well. If you're preparing to lead an RES or Acorn team for the first time, I strongly recommend calling someone who's done—or is doing—the same thing. Most of the people who have these roles are eager to share what they've learned with people in noncompeting companies, precisely because it is so very difficult. There're aren't just droves and hordes of us out there, and I've found quite a lot of camaraderie amongst chief innovation officers, the people who are tasked with incubation, and those heading up entrepreneurial efforts inside organizations.

WEAR A HELMET

I love what I do. I get excited by ideas and imagine multiple possibilities. I enjoy entrepreneurship, but when I'm in the trenches, I wonder if there isn't a certain amount of willful amnesia involved in my enthusiasm. The Acorn Method sounds easy. And I do believe using the structures, process, and strategies it sets out makes building new businesses inside a business less arduous than it would be any other way. But it's still not easy, and I want to acknowledge that. You're going to bang your head against innumerable walls. You're going to get punched in the face. That's what you sign up for when you step on this growing field. I can't tell you how to avoid the hits, only that I believe they're well worth taking.

THINK FAST

As an entrepreneur, perhaps the most powerful weapon you have is the ability, with incomplete information, to make good decisions quickly and, when you have to choose, to pick quick over good. A bad decision is better than no decision or a good decision made too late. If you don't have—and practice—the habit of moving very rapidly from doubt to decision to action, nothing happens. Momentum gets lost. The people you need to persuade get bored and move on. You burn through resources trying to optimize your plan, and have nothing left to fuel executing on it. You wait for clarifying data that doesn't clarify, and end up without clarity or time. The future is uncertain and it changes depending on what you do in the present. Work less on trying to see over the horizon, and more on creating what you want to see when you get there.

In the same way that the life cycles of products and companies are getting shorter and shorter, so are the half-lives of those skills required to be a productive team member. Learning to run experiments, adjust, adapt, and experiment again is an incredibly valuable—and maybe the only truly necessary—skill. It's how you learn how to learn better.

In a professional landscape where things move so quickly that you need to be constantly learning in order to stay relevant, experimentation is a true superpower. Anything that can be taught and automated can, in theory, be replaced by a computer. Building experimentation-iteration loops is a complex skill that's difficult to learn, and even harder to master. It's also almost impossible to replace. Being an entrepreneurial person inside an organization and knowing how to build new businesses there is a very powerful position to occupy. And enjoy.

Before You Put Down This Book and Start Building

Today, mature companies hold onto their dominance for an ever-shrinking length of time. and face unprecedented pressure from shortening product life cycles and expanding fields of competition. Additionally, they are, like tall trees, vertically constrained. The Acorn Method offers businesses a structure, a process, and a strategy for creating something from nothing to get growing again, taking its inspiration from perhaps the most successful species of tree. Here, I'm inspired by another great success. Amazon, according to its founder Jeff Bezos, understands that:

Even though we have some big businesses, new businesses

start up small. It would be very easy for, say, the person who runs the US book category to say, "Why are we doing these experiments with things, I mean, that generated a tiny bit of revenue last year?" But instead inside Amazon, when a new business reaches some small milestone of sales, email messages go out, and everybody gives virtual high fives for reaching that milestone. I think it's because we know from our past experiences, big things start small. The biggest oak starts from an acorn, and if you want to do anything new, you've got to be willing to let that acorn grow into a little sapling, and then finally into a small tree, and maybe one day it'll be a big business on its own.

Because their upward growth slows as they mature, the Acorn Method teaches companies to create a new structure—a Revenue Exploration Studio—in which new, rapid-growth, revenue-producing ventures are continuously developed into an expanding and regenerative portfolio of new businesses.

This development follows an experience-tested, four-step growth process. First, interesting problems are identified within four areas where the company has permission to play. These problems are then reframed to create actionable business ideas several of which are rapidly developed and articulated in the form of a Quick Pitch in step 2. The best Quick Pitches move forward into step 3, the creation of a Lean Product Plan (LPP).

Professionally designed, well-rehearsed and presented to key stakeholders, the LPP makes its most compelling case with the goal of securing time and funding to complete the final process step: Signal Mining. Signal reduces the cost of trying by validating the LPP's key assumptions about revenue, customers and demand.

The Acorn Method's process gives company-sponsored new ventures every advantage, and its strategic component positions them to maximize their launch chances and minimize the sponsor's risk. The first strategy builds a secure runway at the ideal proximity from the parent company, and accounts for the legal and financial relationships between them. The second strategy guides decision-making and next steps at the runway's end.

It's my hope that the Acorn Method has convinced you how necessary (and exciting) it is for mature organizations to get into the business of building new businesses, and has inspired and equipped you to get started doing just that.

We need you to.

Small businesses may form the backbone of most good economies, but we also need mature companies to get growing again. If they don't, they'll be out-competed by both startups and big tech companies. Customers are better served and innovation thrives where there's active competition among a diverse set of players. We need both larger, established organizations and hot new ones to grow a towering, vibrant, sustainable future for us all and, as the proverb runs, "Mighty oaks from little acorns grow."

Additionally, growing Acorns is one of the best things you can do to futureproof your career. The ability to identify a problem, to experiment and solve it in a scalable way is, for me, the core skill every one of us—Fortune 500 CEO and aspiring entrepreneur alike—is going to need in a future of AI, global competition, and robotics. Even more importantly, it's fun! Seeing your ideas materialize quickly is a fantastic high, and making an impact is deeply rewarding.

The Acorn Method is an invitation and a challenge to find, in yourself and in your organization, the perhaps dormant generative impulse, and get it growing again. Your customers, clients, and teams need you to challenge the limiting vertical-only growth paradigm and to create both internal stability *and* internal disruption.

If you're willing to tap the deep roots of creative and entrepreneurial talent, to branch out beyond the expected and into new areas of opportunity, to grow—grounded in solid funding and governance practices—from oak to acorn, Acorn to spun-in or spun-out new venture, the Acorn Method and I are here to help. I hope you'll reach out to me through Twitter (@werdelin) or on LinkedIn as you implement this structure, process, and strategy. I think you'll find the Acorn Method both flexible and strong. Whether you head a mature organization or are just putting out your first new business offshoot, I hope you'll continue to grow, to regrow, and to reach broadly as well as high.

About the Author

HENRIK WERDELIN is the co-founder of America's fastest growing pet brand BARK (makers of BarkBox) and is founding partner of Prehype, an international organization that helps entrepreneurs and companies build new ventures. Henrik has been part of startups that were acquired by Facebook and Microsoft, and has advised companies like Coca-Cola, LEGO, Novozymes, CitiGroup, Intel, Carlsberg, Leo Pharma, and Verizon. His methods are taught at Stanford and other leading universities and have been featured in *Harvard Business Review*, *Bloomberg*, *Fast Company* and other major publications. Originally from Denmark, Henrik lives in New York with his family.